A PRE-MODERNIST MANIFESTO

To John, I hope you
find this more interesting
that Local Development
Plans !!!
Best Wishes,
Mike.

GW00496936

d.

1

A PRE-MODERNIST MANIFESTO

Poetry
and
Prose
for
Pleasure,
Pain
and
Profit

MIKE PANTLING

Matador
9 Priory Business Park,
Wistow Road, Kibworth Beauchamp,
Leicestershire. LE8 0RX
Tel: (+44) 116 279 2299
Fax: (+44) 116 279 2277
Email: books@troubador.co.uk
Web: www.troubador.co.uk/matador

ISBN 978 1784623 647

British Library Cataloguing in Publication Data.
A catalogue record for this book is available from the British Library.

Printed and bound in the UK by TJ International, Padstow, Cornwall
Typeset in Adobe Garamond Pro by Troubador Publishing Ltd, Leicester, UK

Matador is an imprint of Troubador Publishing Ltd

For Gloria; for Julie, Ian and Rebecca; for Andrew, Amanda and David; for James, Georgia and Laura; and for all other family members, whether at home or abroad.

For the memory of Victoria, who would have loved this book.

And for all who love their fellow-men, and who would reach out to them through literature.

CONTENTS

AUTHOR'S PREFACE

The title of this volume states that it should be seen as a Pre-Modernist Manifesto, the word 'manifesto' being particularly apposite in the context of the impending General Election. But it is additionally appropriate because it relates to the ideas and beliefs which underpin this volume. I have become convinced that the many developments since the start of the twentieth century which are known in cultural studies as 'modernity' have brought trends which have harmed the ways in which both English and History are now taught in our schools. This Preface shows how I have acquired this belief, and is written in the hope that if enough people can be persuaded to adopt a more critical approach to the thinking of successive governments in these areas, then it might be possible to recapture some of the ground which has already been lost.

I have described these poems as 'Pre-Modernist' because they illustrate techniques which increasingly fell out of favour as the twentieth century progressed. They were originally designed as a single work which would provide a practical demonstration of the relationship between form and content through the general principle of 'fitness for purpose', and would rely for their effects on traditional poetic devices such as rhythm and rhyme. This aim has remained unchanged, but it has become clear that the distinction between poems for pleasure, for pain and for profit may be very difficult to apply in specific cases, while the verse forms and the contents of the two poems for profit are so different from the others that it seems more appropriate to keep them separate. Hence, although the completed work has been kept in one Volume there are two distinct Books within it, the second having an Introduction which is specific to itself.

It is in our nature as human beings that our basic motivations often reflect a conflict between our hearts and our heads – between what we feel and what we think – between our emotions on the one side and our reason on the other. This dichotomy may be to some extent artificial, but nevertheless, both in itself and in its resolution, it has been the source of great literature of all kinds, and is one element in that 'poetic fancy' and/or 'imagination' about which so much has been written. The shorter poems which form Book One are primarily for the heart, and have been classified into two groups on the basis of their content and anticipated responses to that content. I hope that the poems found in the first part will evoke in the reader, reciter or listener pleasurable feelings or emotions of some kind. Those in Part Two are also mainly for the heart, but they are concerned with themes and situations which are pathetic or tragic, and I hope that those who are moved by them will find a source of solace and strength for those moments when we are forced to confront events and circumstances which we would normally push to the backs of our minds. I would, though, reiterate that the distinction between poems for pleasure, for pain and for profit is somewhat artificial, and would point out that much poetry may simultaneously be seen as both a celebration of and as a crutch for life, a point which was long ago beautifully illustrated by Elizabeth Barrett Browning in her sonnet *Consolation*:

All are not taken; there are left behind
Living Beloveds, tender looks to bring
And make the daylight still a happy thing …

Nearly all the shorter poems may be said to be autobiographical in that they originate in my own direct experiences, or were written to or for other members of our family. As they are essentially self-explanatory and involve themes which are universal, they should initially be approached on their own terms – in a vacuum, as it were. However, each has been given a prose commentary which can be subsequently consulted so that the context of an individual poem is fully accessible. Occasionally, the commentaries have also been used to complement the Introduction to Book Two by providing insights into the creative process. It is hoped that this will deepen the understanding of readers who may lack a formal training in poetics, and will encourage and help any who may wish to know how to appraise different poems and perhaps to experiment in writing their own.

There are already many good books devoted to this, and they vary from the relatively simple (e.g. *An Introduction to English Poetry* by James Fenton, Viking, 2002) to the more advanced (e.g. *The Ode Less Travelled* by Stephen Fry, Hutchinson, 2005). But neither of these authors includes detailed examples showing the construction of their own poems, and Stephen Fry wrote that he thought his readers would be relieved that he was including only samples of his verse specifically designed to clarify form and metre. I class myself as one who was disappointed by this stance, and it is another reason for publishing the commentaries on my own work. Discerning readers will realise that I have used only a small number of standard recognised forms, including blank and heroic verse, the sonnet, and the ballad, and that these were chosen because I deemed them fit for my purposes. I have not tried to write examples of any other recognised forms, partly because none was thought appropriate, and partly because I do not share the view that a form found beautiful in one language will necessarily be found beautiful in another. Neither have I tried to include a glossary of poetic terms. Both books already cited contain formidable lists of their own, and I have worked on a simple 'need to know' basis. Conversely, though, I have included a wide variation in my explanations of both the mechanics and the context of individual poems: while all have been made fully accessible, some have also been given a lengthy analysis which might take in their title, vocabulary, metre, rhyme scheme, line length, the number and length of their stanzas, and any external references or allusions that they might contain. Additionally, I have included a discussion of Italian and English sonnets under *James the First*, and of ballads under *The Ghost of the Ancient Mariner*.

My poems may also be seen as Pre-Modernist because they show that I have little sympathy with those who believe that the imposition of structure and discipline is inimical to creativity; or that poetry can be manufactured from disconnected and chopped-up prose; or that memorable poetry can be written without any attempt to utilise either metre or rhyme, or both. I have no wish to attack or to denigrate those who find pleasure in free verse, futurism, modernism, post-modernism, prose poetry, 'concrete poetry', 'found poetry' or any other writing which attempts to push back the frontiers formed by literary conventions. However, I cannot forbear from pointing out that a potential readership has also been on the receiving end of this pushing, so that as early as 1932 F. R. Leavis could begin *New Bearings in English Poetry* (Chatto and Windus) with the claim that 'poetry matters little to the modern world', and it has been estimated that at present about 90% of the poetry bought by the general public is that written by poets long dead. It may be surmised that most consumers believe that supplying their own titles and/or punctuation, and having to decide whether a poem has a meaning and, if so, to then decipher it, form considerable barriers to enjoyment. Further, few consumers possess the photographic memories necessary to remember long passages of poetry where mnemonic devices have had a low priority; where meaning is vague or obscure; and where stanzas appear to have been devised arbitrarily, having little relationship with either meaning or conventional prosody. Other consumers may be unimpressed by poems presented as geometric shapes or patterns; by those incorporating mathematical symbols or algebraic equations; and, more recently, by those simulating 'computer-speak' or 'text-messaging'. Such poems too often raise artificial barriers to their immediate comprehension and enjoyment, and too often give the impression that the form is more important than the content. Many intelligent consumers have realised that buying such poetry merely encourages the production of more of the same, and hence it is now commonplace that more and more mainstream publishers have abandoned most modernist poets in the belief that they would sell only to other modernist poets.

The two poems found in Book Two of this work are written as much for the head as for the heart, and it is envisaged that any 'profit' derived from them will be primarily intellectual, arising from reading and re-reading rather than from listening. These poems have been written specifically with a view to publication, and reflect my lifelong interest in both poetry and history, exploring what might be termed the philosophy or politics of the latter through the medium of verse rather than the more customary prose. My interest was first crystallised in 1961 when J. M. Cameron, a philosopher and one of my former tutors, analysed the ways in which truth as a concept might be applied to poetry. He quoted Aristotle as remarking that Herodotus put into verse would still be history and not poetry, and as claiming that 'poetry is something more philosophic and of graver import than history'. Many years later, in 1987, 1 had occasion to read the Preface which Wordsworth had written in 1800 for the Second Edition of *Lyrical Ballads*. He cited Aristotle with approval, contending that 'the obstacles which stand in the way of the fidelity of the Biographer and Historian, and of their consequent utility, are incalculably greater than those which are to be encountered by the Poet who comprehends the dignity of his art'; and he implied that the 'truth' which he believed is the natural possession of poets as human beings is of a superior class to that recovered by biographers and historians, since 'poetry is the first and last of all knowledge'. I find these views mistaken, but they have been given a wide currency since the early nineteenth century, and in an extended form have helped to produce a situation where it appears that any form of creative writing may be classed as poetry, including even that which appears as prose. Today, there are those who will accept my long poems as verse but who will deny that they are poetry on the grounds that the contents are 'not poetical'. Hence, I am including as an introduction to these poems a discursive rationale for both their contents and their forms, though it is not necessary to study this before enjoying the poems themselves. Here I need only state that they endorse the presumption of the Ancient Greeks that poetry is a proper medium for serious and philosophic subjects, and that they combine this idea with overall structures and verse forms which allow the incorporation of concepts and vocabulary which are today taken for granted within educated circles in general, and within the social sciences in particular. Experimentation showed that this required not only a tight conceptual framework but also highly disciplined verse forms which would accord with the former yet still allow a degree of variety and a high level of instant comprehension. Both poems are designed to be enjoyed either as a whole or within their respective constituent parts. However, as they both contain a large amount of didactic material, the reader should repeatedly stop to think about what has been read, and hence reasoning processes should be the precursors and determinants of any subsequent emotional responses.

I was already perplexed by what was passing for modern

poetry when I went up to Leeds University in 1958, and while there I had several inconclusive one-to-one discussions with Jon Silkin on the subject. Then, in 1963, I was given a copy of 'archy & mehitabel' by Don Marquis, and this led me to abandon poetry for the duration. I resumed both reading and writing it in 1981, as part of my coming to terms with the accidental death of one of the daughters of close friends. In 1997 I submitted a poem to Hamilton and Company who were advertising for a projected anthology for St. Valentine's Day. Their anthology was eventually aborted, but I will always be grateful to them for the personal interest they took in my work from 1998 to 2002, when they went out of business. They encouraged me to write in both poetry and prose, and were particularly keen that I should complete my long poem on the coal-mining industry in the early nineteenth century. Hence, I became a subscriber to *Writing Magazine* in January 1998; have since followed anything they have published on poetry with great interest; and was delighted when an earlier version of one of my sonnets won one of their poetry prizes and was featured with a detailed critique in the *Annual Competitions Guide* for 2006-7. There has been much discussion on the subject of rhyming poetry versus free verse in the letters pages of both *Writers' News* – now absorbed into *Writing Magazine* – and *Writing Magazine*, particularly from 2003 onwards. In October 2004, Alison Chisholm, their leading expert and adjudicator, replied to a correspondent who had failed to gain any understanding or inspiration from the poems selected by the Academi judges for that year's awards. She stated that 'the past hundred years or so have brought about huge changes in the definition of poetry, allowing free verse, with or without metre, to stand with equal status alongside rhymed poetry and traditional patterns'. In May 2005, the *News* published a letter from myself in which I pointed out that the winning poem in the recent Arvon International Poetry Competition might be seen as a laudable piece of creative writing but it was not a poem. I also complained that the traditional sonnet seemed to be in danger. The *News* itself carried an article in February 2007 on page 58 headed *What is poetry?*. Alison stated that it 'is defined and understood in different ways by different people, and dictionary definitions can't really encompass the depth of the word'. It seems that neither she nor her then colleagues (Doris Corti and Peggy Poole) believe that metre is an essential part of poetry, and all three experts produced definitions or characteristics which could equally well apply to good prose. Hence, my discussion in the Introduction to Book Two of what poetry meant to both Aristotle and Wordsworth is not only to shed light on the form and content of my long poems: it is also to stimulate discussion on whether the word 'poetry' should be restored to its major historical use, namely a form of oral or written communication which replaces speech and prose rhythm by verse metre, with or without rhyme.

Alongside the extension of the word poetry to include writings in prose there have been equally spurious attempts to restrict its appellations. Didactic poetry in particular has been increasingly downgraded as mere versification and its contents dismissed as mere preaching, attitudes which betray a distressing lack of sympathy with English poetry as it has evolved over the centuries. The approximately 30,000 lines of surviving Anglo-Saxon poetry reflect the interests of the church and of the nobility who controlled the institutions producing the written word: hence, most of it is of a religious, historical, homiletic and aphoristic nature, its primary purpose being didactic. This desire to use poetry for instruction continued down the ages along with increased secularisation and more attention to geography, industry and trade: by the end of the eighteenth century, examples included poems devoted to the early history of the steam engine, the textile trades, the Isle of Wight, and the topography around Birmingham. While much of this verse may have been of poor quality, it sometimes served its purpose admirably. Thus, for example, Erasmus Darwin wanted 'to enlist the imagination under the banner of science', and the historian R. J. White claimed in *The Age of George III* (Heinemann, London, 1968, p. 150) that 'there is no better, or more enlivening, way of discovering the exact state of science and technology in the last decade of the eighteenth century than from the text and notes of *The Botanic Garden*, published in two parts in 1789 and 1791 respectively, and reprinted four times before the end of the century'. Over our history, then, poetry embraced a wide and generous tradition, and it was argued by E. C. Batho and B. Dobrée in *The Victorians And After* (Cresset Press, London, 1938) that the second most important characteristic of poets from the 1830s to the 1880s was the feeling that they had an immediate mission, and ought to utter a message. As for the readers, 'they did not mind, it would appear, whether poetry was present or not, so long as they got the doctrine, the revelation, or the interpretation'. Astonishingly, the authors condemn both sides for 'introducing an alien element into poetry', a silly charge that would have amazed the Victorians and which could only have originated in the modernist and unhistorical definition that emerged in the early years of the twentieth century (Ibid, p. 41-2).

There were at least two factors which were instrumental in encouraging a shift away from didactic poetry. The spread of Romanticism among the literary classes was accompanied by a strong distaste for industrialisation and its associated problems, and this began to be reflected in the anthologies that were produced for a widening market. Unfortunately, these fostered a prejudice against long poems, many of which were didactic in nature. The two most successful anthologies were probably Francis Turner Palgrave's *Golden Treasury*, first published in 1861, and the original *Oxford Book of English Verse*, first edited in 1900 by Arthur Quiller-Couch. Palgrave wanted only lyrics and songs, and he banished narrative, descriptive and didactic poems. Quiller-Couch argued that the best English poems were either lyrical or epigrammatic, though the latter must have some degree of emotional input. Similarly, Thomas Caldwell, whose *Golden Book of Modern English Poetry* covered the years from the 1870s to the 1920s, believed that the best poetry was either classical or romantic in character. He was particularly against poetry of the 'realistic school', and his Preface to the 1930 edition states that such poetry 'could not maintain the tradition of form and beauty'. The Introduction by Lord Dunsany supports this theme at more length, and the volume as a whole supports the views of Palgrave and Quiller-Couch.

The second, and probably the biggest, influence in

fostering the low repute of didactic poetry was the conception promulgated by the followers of Wordsworth. Their ideas slowly but surely infiltrated the older grammar schools and began to dominate the developing national system of education, and particularly the work of the colleges set up for the training of teachers. Our mother attended the Girls' High School in Lincoln where she spent not less than a year in the mid-1920s studying Wordsworth's poetry and prose. Our father entered St John's College, York, in 1929, and we still possess some of the textbooks that were then used to instruct students in the teaching of English. If these can be taken as representative, they show that Wordsworth's views on what poetry should be and on how it should be evaluated had won over the educational establishment, and were being used to influence a whole generation of teachers and hence also their pupils. E. A. Greening Lamborn, in *The Rudiments of Criticism* (Oxford, 1916) referred in his Preface to 'the fatal error of reading poetry for the substance and not for the form of its matter', devoted his first chapter to defining poetry, and subsequently heaped praise on Wordsworth's own prose prefaces, repeatedly contending that 'men want to be made to feel, not made to think' (pp 1-2; pp 119-120). Lamborn wrote the Preface for W. S. Tomkinson's *The Teaching of English: A New Approach* (Oxford, 1921), which on page 52 included the following:

> 'The page of the man of science is an instance of the use of language for information: the page of the poet, and often the prose artist, is an instance of the use of the language of emotion, and didactic poetry

> does not destroy this distinction, since it is a poetic
> changeling and not of the true stock.'

In his last chapter Tomkinson stated that 'emotion and not reason takes the initiative, and always colours the thought. Works of art are not mere matters of fact, and the cognitive aspect is of secondary importance' (p. 182). Similar sentiments are to be found in Robert Finch's *How to Teach English Composition* (Evans Bros., London,) and in G. E. Hollingworth's *Primer of Literary Criticism* (University Tutorial Press, London, 1930). I have examined Wordsworth's views in my introduction to Book 2, where I show that he must shoulder some of the blame for the subsequent prejudice against didactic poetry and especially against writers like Crabbe and Pope who were increasingly accused of being mere versifiers or inferior 'poetasters' rather than true poets.

My long poems are thus a reversion to, and a practical defence of, a very ancient but now marginalised tradition, and I believe that they are completely original within it. However, as they differ greatly from each other in both conception and execution they are best considered individually.

A Vindication of Early Miners is a wholly didactic poem that for the most part many of the Radical leaders of the first half of the nineteenth century would have understood, loved, reprinted and recited at their meetings. It should be remembered that much English socialist writing already existed in the 1820s, or long before any influence exercised by Marx and Engels. The leaders of the embryonic trade unions, early co-operatives, and of the Chartists in the 1840s would have found nothing strange about the economic and political analysis involved in this *Vindication*, the only exception being my discussion of the quantitative techniques used by modern historians. The remaining content is what they themselves were preaching, although many of them would have included a justification of the then current Labour Theory of Value. This argued that the true source of all increases in wealth was the productive labour of the wage-earner, and it therefore repudiated the claims of other classes to rents, interest and profits.

The second long poem, *The Only Dreamscape History Of The Early English State In Verse*, is a hybrid which combines fact and fiction. Part One, providing the justification for the Dreamscapes, examines the problems involved in the writing of academic history. It is overwhelmingly didactic, and puts into verse many of the issues normally found in texts covering the use and abuse of sources in the search for historical truth. It should particularly appeal to anyone interested in the place of history in the educational system, and especially in the controversies respecting the content of a national curriculum and the methods of examining it. Part Two, in contrast, is wholly a work of imagination. It uses the old literary devices of a dream and a narrator/guide to introduce a fantasy in which a substantial core of established historical fact and generalisations concerning the nature of early English society are mixed with fabrications, myths, anachronisms and insights from the social sciences to produce a coherent account of the origins of the English state and class structure and its accompanying distribution of power and wealth.

While there exists an abundance of poems dealing with particular aspects and events of English history, as far as I know this work is unique in both conception and execution.

Both these long poems reflect the overall impression derived from a professional life spent in researching, teaching and examining in history. They are one product of my increasing disillusionment at the ever-widening gap between history as conceived of by professional or 'academic' historians and history as conceived of by society in general, the latter of course being the principal consumers as well as financiers of the subject. The search for truth within the ivory towers has too often led merely to a multiplicity of conflicting and often inconsequential truths, while the more esoteric writings on the methods and philosophy of the subject have given credence to the view that there is no such thing as historical truth anyway. Thus, the apparent health of the subject as evinced in society's increased preoccupation with all things historical and in its rôle in the tourism and leisure industry has served to disguise the unpalatable fact that its original and indispensable content has been downgraded. As a result, millions of our children are now being deprived of an historical and cultural legacy about which they display an innate curiosity from an early age, and to which they have an entitlement as future citizens.

The blame for this most lamentable state of affairs must be placed squarely on the shoulders of both practitioners and educationalists. Academics are guilty because they have lost sight of and faith in their essential core, and are now unable to discriminate between what is important and what is peripheral in their subject matter. Consequently, they have fallen into the trap of justifying their subject not in terms of what it contains, but in terms of the skills that are developed by studying it. In this they have been aided and abetted by those whose functionalist approach belies the very name of educationalists. Their utilitarian and cost-effective criteria have been readily matched to the hierarchy of skills they think essential for a trained workforce, and which the study of history can help to develop. Thus, the abilities to empathise and to critically examine and then draw conclusions from evidence have been deemed more important than historical knowledge or facts in themselves, which are seen as 'useless' or 'irrelevant' or 'boring' or 'one damn thing after another'. This view suits their other purpose, since the more intelligent among them are aware that historical facts can be dangerous facts, and that those who can assimilate, remember and interpret them meaningfully can be dangerous people – especially dangerous to those who would pervert the said facts for their own purposes.

Recently, Jeremy Paxman suggested that poetry has connived at its own irrelevance, and that this should not happen because it's 'a most delightful thing'. He thought that very often poets seem to be talking only to other poets rather than to people as a whole. Similarly, *Writing Magazine* for September and October 2014 carried five letters which taken as a totality praised rhythm and rhyme and lamented that most free verse seemed unpoetical and often incomprehensible. My volume should please both Jeremy and the letter-writers. Additionally, it is the product of a cultural heritage which pre-dates 'dumbing-down' and 'political correctness'. I find it greatly disturbing that, in all probability, the book which most inspired my own love of poetry while I was at primary school would not be published today, since it bears what would now be perceived as the highly challenging title of *One Hundred Poems for Boys*. If my volume should either give pleasure or soothe pain, then that would be sufficient justification for the effort I have put into it. But if it should additionally give both profit and pause to those who seem to have forgotten why as a society and as individuals we need both poetry and prose, and why our children need to be taught the existence and appreciation of a literary canon and a meaningful chronological history of their own country, then this would give me even greater satisfaction.

Thomas Hood wished that his epitaph should record him as the composer of *The Song of the Shirt*, a judgement on his overall output from which I for one would not dissent. There are times, however, when I would prefer to re-read his *Faithless Nelly Gray*, for I know of no other poem of similar length which contains a greater amount of sustained humour, especially punning. This demonstrates that for me both the writing and reading of poetry are mainly a matter of mood, and I suspect that this is true of a great majority of poetry-lovers. The acid test of any collection is whether it is one to which readers would wish to return, either in whole or in part, again and again. Should there prove to be such readers of my volume, they will find that individual poems and passages may be easily retrieved, and that in general the poetry itself is not difficult to memorise, if that is what is desired. And if I were to follow the example of Thomas

Hood, I would want my epitaph to record me as the author of the sonnet, *Your Father's Last Wish*. I believe that I will never write a finer poem than this, and I hope that, as my own father and mother are always with me, so my wife and myself will always be with our children.

Michael John Pantling – January, 2015.

PART ONE

POEMS FOR PLEASURE

POEMS FOR PLEASURE

1. In Defence of Lyric Poets: A Reply to the Love
       Song of J. Alfred Prufrock
2. To Gloria, my Love
3. Returning Home after Haymaking
4. Our Ken, our Hero
5. A Poem for Rebecca's Seventeenth Christmas
6. Wedding Jitters
7. James the First
8. James the Second
9. A Fishy Tale
10. The Ghost of the Ancient Mariner
11. Is this the Face?
12. Cogito, ergo sum.

IN DEFENCE OF LYRIC POETS

A REPLY TO THE LOVE SONG OF J. ALFRED
PRUFROCK (T. S. ELIOT, 1917)

We'll not be going anywhere at all.
There'll never ever be a you and me,
And I'm appalled that you should have the gall
To think I'd want to share your misery.
I'd rather eat a trillion thrice-dried prunes
Than measure out my life with coffee spoons;
And I believe you should remain unwed –
Your heart will never overrule your head,
And, though alive, you might as well be dead.
But I'm in thrall to poets from former times,
Who seduced me with sweet words,
And charmed me with their rhymes.

Praise poets who sing of matchless maids
Walking in beauty within glades;
Or shepherdesses and their swains,
Courting in leafy country lanes.

There's no rapture in your affirmation.
There is a strange inordinate concern
For fog, and smoke, and soot, and stagnant drains –
For things a normal lyric poet disdains.
And images of disembodied heads,

Or patients on a table etherised,
Or specimens both pinned and traumatised,
Or silent, sea-bound, scuttling, ragged claws,
Do little to promote a lover's cause.
Why can't you be like poets from former times,
Who delight with sweet, sweet words,
And woo with soothing rhymes?

> *Laud those who find in their love's face*
> *All flowers that may a garden grace;*
> *Or else a rare and precious stone,*
> *With a perfection all its own.*

You only show your troubled state of mind,
And that self-pity to which you're inclined.
You're full of 'ifs' and 'buts' and 'hows' and 'whys'
To which your gnawing intellect gives rise,
And with which you will ever agonise.
Your love's for 'victim syndrome'. It's so strong
It overwhelms the tenor of your song,
And it's dragging you from mild obsession
Into formal clinical depression.
You can't compare with poets from former times,
Who beguile with sweet, sweet words,
And lull with soothing rhymes.

> *Hail those who write of slender hips,*
> *Of rosy cheeks, and trembling lips;*
> *And golden hair which tumbles down*
> *To lustrous eyes of wide renown.*

A life with you I really could not bear.
Why should I trust a man who takes such care
In making up the latest mask he'll wear?
Why share my deepest feelings with this man,
When he'll return as little as he can?
Why take for husband one who cannot give
That hope eternal by which humans live?
And why play deaf to everything with voice,
When all too soon death will remove that choice?
Open your heart like poets from former times,
Who bewitch with sweet, sweet words,
And tempt with soothing rhymes.

> *Cheer those who would compare their love*
> *To sun, or moon, or stars above;*
> *And those who try to count the ways*
> *Their love consumes their nights and days.*

You claim that mermaids will not sing for you.
Yet sing they do, though you've stopped up your ears
With wax made firm through fasts and prayers and tears
Which serve to further fuel your inner fears.
O miserable man, your God to scan!
Why can't your worrying intellect accept
Those two commandments which your Saviour kept?
First you must learn to trust your God, and then
You'll love both living and your fellow men.
Forsake modernity! Hymn former times!
Gladly welcome honeyed words,
And use the power of rhymes.

So, Thomas, I can live without
Your life of endless, joyless, doubt.
I'll find a lyricist who sings
Those harmonies which true love brings,
And each new morning I'll rejoice
When I first hear his human voice.

IN DEFENCE OF LYRIC POETS

A REPLY TO THE LOVE SONG OF J. ALFRED
PRUFROCK (T.S. ELIOT, 1917)

T. S. Eliot's poem was published in 1917, and I was introduced to it while I was in the sixth form. I did not understand it then, and today, older and more knowledgeable, and after many more readings, I continue to doubt whether I have fully mastered it. What I do not doubt is that it gives me very little pleasure, and that this is primarily because, on my interpretation, it is both egocentric in conception and life-denying in its thrust – two qualities antithetical to the 'Love Song' claimed in the title. I have no objection in principle to poems which, using Eliot's own word, are 'difficult', but without clarification such poems risk being misunderstood. A more recent copy of this poem can be found in *The New Oxford Book of English Verse* (1972, pp. 873-876).

The 'Reply' assumes that Prufrock is unmarried; imagines that I am the female recipient of his devotion; and contains changes in form which reflect the movements within it from declamation to lyricism and vice versa. It begins by maintaining the traditional pentameter, but the longer stanzas are completed by a triplet in which the syllable count (10, 7, 6) is used to slow the rhythm, while the rhyme scheme (A, B, A) and partial repetition signal the end of the stanzas themselves. The whole effect thus prepares for the changeover and, subsequently, the addition of two lines to the last stanza through a rhyming couplet is used to close the poem.

With respect to the content, Eliot's references to 'an overwhelming question' (lines 10 and 93), to Hamlet himself (line 111) and to Hamlet's attendant lord (line 112), indicate that the 'question' itself is Hamlet's 'To be, or not to be?'. My own lines 5 and 6 originate in the oft-quoted, 'I have measured out my life with coffee spoons' (line 51); and most of the other material used in the rebuttal is scattered around the original poem. My lyrical verses differ from the others in that they allude to other much admired poems from the pre-modernist tradition. These begin with the anonymous carol, 'I sing of a maiden that is makeles' (the latter word being conventionally modernised as 'matchless'), and include 'She walks in beauty, like the night' from Lord Byron, and 'How do I love thee? Let me count the ways' from Elizabeth Barrett Browning. The expression, 'hope springs eternal', originates with Pope. 'Love God' and 'Love thy neighbour as thyself' are recognised as all-important by the Church of England, which teaches that 'there is no other commandment greater than these: upon these two commandments hang all the law and the prophets'. My reference to 'Doubting Thomas' (lines 77-78) includes both Prufrock and Thomas Stearns Eliot. The concluding stanza is a response to Eliot's own last line, which reads: 'Till human voices wake us, and we drown'.

Overall, my poem is to be seen as a defence of the traditional English love poem, and as a repudiation of many of the developments now associated with modernity, particularly the exclusiveness of the poetry but also the right-wing political views of writers like Eliot and Pound. It is a reminder that love is an integral part of our common humanity, and an area where so-called intellectuals have no claim to any superiority, since the possession of a Leavis-like 'adult sensitive mind' is not a prerequisite for the possession of human sympathies or the formation of human relationships. The poem is a political as well as a poetical manifesto: it reflects my view as a life-long Labour activist that one should 'take arms against a sea of troubles and by opposing, end them', and that weeping and wailing or 'washing one's hands like Pilate' will do little to improve the general condition of mankind.

TO GLORIA, MY LOVE

Please don't see your engagement ring
In values vaunting vendors use.
Don't slight its stone as some mean thing
That's often spurned when others choose.
But rather, darling, you should view
This symbol I've reserved for you
As representing things we've prized
Which never could be realised.

So when this ring you idly twirl,
Reflect upon a former time,
And picture one who loved a girl
His poet's heart had deemed sublime.
Recall him working day by day –
The extra hours – the lowly pay –
And how he scrimped and scraped and saved
To deck the hand for which he craved.

And let the purple of the stone
Remind you of his vassal state.
And let the amethyst alone
His drunken passion temperate.
Then, as your reverie you close,
Look fondly on this ring he chose,
And, darling, know you can be sure
You'll stay my love for evermore.

TO GLORIA, MY LOVE

This is one result of a previous media quest to find the nation's favourite love poems, and of my wife's suggestion that she would like one of her own, addressed to her personally. I believe I am right in thinking that this is now her most treasured poem. It rhymes, it scans, and it is easily memorised, but both the content and the language require some explanation if the poem is to be fully accessible to, and appreciated by, others.

Taking the content first, the second verse relates to the fact that in the six months prior to our formal engagement in April 1965 I was employed as an unskilled factory worker. My basic wage was then one penny under £10 per week, but was augmented by a productivity bonus and by weekend working. The ring was bought from a small antiques shop in Leeds and in cost was equivalent to about two weeks' wages.

Etymologically, love poems present difficulties because the 'language of love' has been handed down to us over the centuries, thus presenting the problem of marrying what is sometimes called 'archaic' or 'poetic' diction with that used today. In this poem, I regard the opening lines as crucial since they determine the tone of the whole poem, but to modernise them might have an intrusively distorting effect. Thus, an early draft of the first line reads: 'Now don't see your engagement ring'. The tone is strident, either hectoring or admonitory, and hence discordant in a love poem. The two lines eventually chosen are more suggestion than admonition, and subsequently alliteration, assonance and rhyme have been used to maintain an appropriate tone. The inversions and archaic words of earlier drafts were also removed in order to give a modern 'feel'.

There are remaining points on the inter-relationships between tone, meaning and vocabulary which should be made. Firstly, the word 'realised' (line 8) has been used in its commercial sense of converting assets into money, such assets including intangibles such as goodwill. The ring as a ring once had a price, probably inflated by the last seller. However, it pre-dates the wedding ring, and has come to symbolise 'the things we've prized' or valued in our life together rather than material things which we could have 'priced'. The former, which have been achieved or 'won' rather than bought, are also intangibles, like a loving family and shared achievements, memories and experiences. For us, therefore, the ring now has an added value that cannot be quantified in monetary terms: it cannot be 'realised' because its 'sentimental value' makes it priceless.

Secondly, 'sublime' (line 12) is the word that has come to be used by both poets and literary critics when describing the highest level to which poetry can aspire. It would be entirely in keeping for a poet to think of his love in this way.

Thirdly, 'deck' (line 16) might be thought archaic, but I think it is justified by the context. Today, as a verb, it is mostly associated with a particular Christmas carol in the line, 'Deck the halls with boughs of holly'. But Christmas is about presents as well as putting up decorations, so that the ring which adorns also symbolises giving.

Fourthly, 'vassal state' (line 18) denotes the historical

connection between purple and power, both civil and ecclesiastical, and the nature of the implied feudal relationship. The colour purple and a ring are symbolic of the power of emperors and bishops, who were the liege lords; and the vassal was in a subordinate position or 'state', pledging his love and his faithfulness even unto death. My position could therefore be said to be similar.

Lastly, 'temperate' (line 20), besides recalling Shakespeare's Sonnet No XVIII ('Shall I compare thee to a summer's day? Thou art more lovely and more temperate'), denotes the fact that many Classical writers believed that amethyst (a form of quartz) had an inhibiting effect on drunkenness. It suggests that the relatively uncontrolled passion of youth, which can be a destructive as well as a constructive force, will be moderated over time into a more serene but deeper form of love.

Overall, this analysis shows the importance of a consistent tone and vocabulary, and demonstrates that even a relatively short poem can carry a wealth of allusions.

RETURNING HOME AFTER HAYMAKING

Sometimes, we'd come back by a horse and cart.
We'd climb up and, sitting on top,
We'd pray that the swaying would stop.
It was scary, moving by cart.
We had to take care not to slip,
And hunt fixings which we could grip.
It was dang'rous, travelling by cart.
And a journey is one long bore
When your toys are just bits of straw.
We'd not want to come back by cart.

Often, we'd come back to the yard on foot.
We'd loiter and, lagging behind,
We'd peer round for things we might find.
We felt safer, dawdling on foot.
And if little feet had to run,
Then that was all part of the fun.
We were happy, skipping on foot.
We'd chase pretend rabbits with sticks,
Play ball, and discover new tricks.
It was great to come back on foot.

RETURNING HOME AFTER HAYMAKING

Romantics often fail to understand many of the realities entailed by a rural childhood in the years before the early 1950s, and too often forget that the playground of the child was often also the workplace of adults. Looking back through the perspective of a 'Health and Safety at Work' society, both my wife and I are astonished at the risks to which we were exposed as infants, she in rural Cumbria and myself in rural Lincolnshire. The poem draws on my memories of the years about 1944-48 (when I had a free run of a neighbour's farmyard), and it attempts to present a child's eye view of what was a fairly common-place experience. It is fully accessible, and a reminder that in those days one could play happily with a whip-and-top down the centre of what was a fairly substantial made-up road. Inside the farmyard, we would slide both hands up the leg of a cart-horse to see how high we could go before our hands would no longer meet. And we would actually sit on the haystacks beside the escalator to help hold the straw in position while the traction engine was running and the stacks were being built.

My rural childhood often involved going out alone at night in the dark, sometimes for a short distance (e.g. to visit the unlit and pail-emptied privy), and sometimes, with or without my brothers, for the longer journeys necessary to change books at the circulation library which visited the school, or to attend choir practice at the local church. Such journeys could produce the occasional terrifying experience, a point to which I return in my later discussion of *The Ghost of the Ancient Mariner*.

OUR KEN, OUR HERO

Though he would visit while the war was on,
We were too little to remember him;
And it would be another thirteen years
Before we saw his face again. And so
We knew him mainly through old photographs;
And fictions family history claims as facts;
And letters written on blue envelopes;
Or presents which were brought by parcel post.
'Par-Av-i-on', and 'Ca-na-da', we'd say,
As we put stamps and atlases away.

Our father was the first-born of three boys.
The photographs he had out on display
Gave equal pride of place to Cliff and Ken
In Army and in Air Force uniform,
With both so handsome, and our Ken so young.
Smiling and spruce, it seemed they would define
Through studio portraits for which they had posed
The final image they would leave behind.
And as Ken's face stayed fixed before our eyes,
He was the easiest to romanticise.

For children need their heroes, and will choose
On grounds which adult minds might find unsound.
Thus, with dad also in the R.A.F.,
The 'senior service' was self-evident.

But dads and land-based aircraftsmen are dull,
Since glory's in the skies. Our Biggles, then,
We found in our own Ken, and hence we'd boast
We'd won the war through men on flying-boats.
And Catalina seemed a splendid name –
One novelists devised to match Ken's fame.

We knew this hero loved us when he sent
Presents with which he'd turn us into men –
The kind of presents parents seldom buy
Lest 'darlings' suffer hurt or injury.
So we got roller skates, and wooden clubs,
And, best of all, a pair of boxing gloves;
And we thought if we were to be like him,
We'd have to learn to take things on the chin.
For heroes have to overcome their fears,
And only cissies are allowed their tears.

So we would be rear-gunners, too. We'd wear
Old flying headgear in winter ice and
Snows, like those who braved inclement weather
On patrol; and, lest one day we needed
Rescuing, we'd study aeroplanes, and
Learn to float and swim. And we'd terrify
Our enemies with 'Tat-tat-tat-tat-tats!'
Or 'Bangs Bangs' made with toy guns and their caps,
When we played out Ken's deeds and derring-do,
Which, over time, just grew, and grew, and grew.

'Civvy Street' could not diminish Ken, whose
Exploits in Toronto swelled as they were
Sifted from his mother and his other
Kin. 'He's married a Canadian' – a
First. 'He's got a telephone' – another
First. 'They've had a baby girl' – a doubtful
First, until our joy when 'This time it's a
Boy'. And then more firsts: 'Ken's got a games-room
Underneath his house', and 'Goodness me, see
His number-plates, with letters K.D.P.'

Thus we as children magnified 'Our Ken',
Who volunteered and served throughout the war,
And was our paragon of manliness.
But when, much grown, and loyalty intact,
We met him face to face, it soon became
Most clear that our conceptions would not bring
Him any cheer. War's not some childish game,
Which he had fought for fun and fame. He'd just
Done his duty, as all around him had:
He was the same as Uncle Cliff and Dad.

He was, of course, quite right. Yet so were we,
For reasons only grownups see. It takes
Great courage to unloosen knots which tie
To family and friends, and to exchange
Familiar spots for foreign soils and all
That fate intends. But that is what be did.

Demobbed in Canada, he built success
On willpower and his own two feet. And that
Is why, though childhood fantasies depart,
He'll always stay a hero in my heart.

OUR KEN, OUR HERO

A s this is an 'heroic' poem, it would normally be written in iambic pentameters and continuous rhyming couplets, with only occasional variations in both the scansion and the rhyme scheme. However, it was apparent that the material would be better broken up into separate stanzas, and so the traditional continuous couplets would be inappropriate. Thus, I decided to use blank verse for the main part of the stanzas but to round them off with a couplet. The syllable count of the pentameters determines the length of the individual lines, while variations in the stresses, a moving caesura, and enjambment within the stanzas help drive the narrative forward. I have held the verse together by the customary devices of full rhymes, slant rhymes, half-rhymes, assonance and consonance. The use of slant rhyme meant that the greatest care had to be taken in matching the sense rhythm to the verse metre, but overall the poem demonstrates how flexible blank verse can be.

In content, the poem continually betrays its era and its origins. This was a world in which most homes would have their studio portraits of service personnel out on display, and where hero-worship was not regarded as a crime and might take in anyone from the war (e.g. Douglas Bader), from the wireless (e.g. Dick Barton, Special Agent), from sport (e.g. Bruce Woodcock from boxing and Len Hutton from cricket) and from comics (e.g. 'Roy of the Rovers' and 'Limp-along

Leslie' – these were in the best buy children's comics, like *Adventure*, *Hotspur* and *Rover*.) It was an era in which for most families the telegram was more important than the telephone, and where bicycles, motorbikes and steam trains were more important than cars. The expression 'Senior Service' was used for a cigarette brand which featured the Royal Navy, the epithet having become customary over the centuries. 'Civvy Street' denoted civilian life. And it is believed that the word 'cissie', meaning an effeminate person, had been popularised by the Americans. The R.A.F. itself was held in great esteem and affection: I remember cycling over to Waddington to see Canberras and Meteors as they came into service. Above all else, our world was a male world. I and both my brothers attended boys' grammar schools. We had a female cousin in Lincoln, but she was older than us and only occasionally contacted. Uncle Cliff had two boys, and when we visited always took us to watch Luton Town. His mother and father taught us various domino and card games, and grandma took us to greyhound races and also taught us how to bet and make the appropriate calculations for horses and the pools.

Uncle Ken (1920-2013) was to outlive his brothers, dying aged ninety-three. Dad (1913-74) had a heart attack in his last term as a headmaster, aged sixty-one. Uncle Cliff (1915-2011) outdid them both, living until he was ninety-six.

A POEM FOR REBECCA'S SEVENTEENTH CHRISTMAS

A mind that's sound has our Rebecca.
She's been grafting at her schoolwork
Now that her exams are near.
She's found out vet schools have high standards,
And that better marks cost dear.
She knows bright suns will black clouds smother,
As old William Shakespeare once made clear.

A generous soul has our Rebecca.
She finds time for little creatures
Who might otherwise be lost.
She loves all sorts of things that wriggle,
And she gives them kindly words,
And when creepy-crawlies don't reply,
She thinks of St. Francis and his birds.

A brave, brave heart has our Rebecca.
She arm-wrestles with her peer group,
Sometimes even beating boys.
And she can eye-ball hands-high horses,
Holding them in gentle thrall,
And jumping them with grit and balance,
Cossack-like, she'll only rarely fall.

A frame that's slight has our Rebecca.
She stands barefoot in the bathroom

Wishing pounds upon her weight.
She hopes that she'll grow much, much taller,
And that broader hips will come,
And she wants platform shoes for Christmas,
As a Lilliputian might have done.

A stride that's long has our Rebecca.
She's a wonder on the sports-field
Racing with more senior girls.
She runs though lacking formal training,
Winning through her talent rude,
And, collecting cups and gaining plaudits,
Seems an Ancient Greek in attitude.

Reddish-gold hair has our Rebecca.
She'll sit upright by her mirror,
Combing out her lovely locks.
And then she'll brush them firmly downwards,
Counting strokes from one to five,
And, tossing curls with gay abandon
Seem our own Boudicca come alive.

Precious to us is our Rebecca.
She's enriched us with her presence
Now for more than sixteen years,
And in that time we've always loved her,
Shared her hopes, and dried her tears.
So, Santa, please, keep your presents dear –
But send us, please, another one like her!

A POEM FOR REBECCA'S
SEVENTEENTH CHRISTMAS

The original version was written as a personal poem for our youngest daughter when she was revising her G.C.S.E. English, and she requested my help with the poetry. Though she knew some rudiments of criticism, she had never actually written any poetry for herself: hence, this poem was designed specifically as a teaching aid.

Composition proved more difficult than I had anticipated, since once the content had been sketched out I found that the form was manifestly influenced by Longfellow's 'Hiawatha', and that further problems arose from the stresses involved in using the name Rebecca. I eventually concluded it should be used only at the beginning of a verse and at the end of a line; that this line should form the introductory line for each verse; and that it should have nine syllables. A verse of seven lines would allow one and perhaps two basic ideas to be developed: thus, lines four, six and seven should match line one in syllable count, with line two being slightly shorter and lines three and five being the shortest. The basic pattern is thus 9, 8, 7, 9, 7, 9 and 9. The rhyme scheme was then established by the first verse, using the endings of lines three, five and seven to set an overall pattern of A, B, C, D, C, E, and C. However, this often proved too strong, so that verses two to six weakened it by dispensing with the rhyme in line three, while the middle verse, verse four, was given a false rhyme. This weakening of the rhyme scheme is more than compensated for by the repetition found within the syntax of the whole poem. The last verse recalls the original pattern by rhyming lines three and five only; by using similar sounds ('years' and 'tears' to recall 'near', 'dear' and 'clear', previously used in verse one); and by re-using 'dear' itself at the end of line six. The poem is rounded off by increasing the number of syllables in the last line to ten, and this line is then used to give additional strength and unity by recalling line four, the same word, 'her', being used at the end of both.

It can be seen that it was necessary to devise a form which would allow a tone of unconditional love to be combined with both admiration and affectionate bemusement. It was also necessary to keep to a modern idiom, and to ensure that the vocabulary and any external references fell within Rebecca's competence.

Two days after completing and taking Rebecca through this poem, I received one back from her. This 'Poem for Dad and His Love of Creatures' is now one of my own treasured possessions. Mission accomplished!

WEDDING JITTERS

Some of our photographs betray
The qualms I suffered on the day
I gave my firstborn child away,
Watching her walk in bridal dress
Towards an untried tenderness.

But later photographs attest
That she's laid all my fears to rest,
And that her loving heart knew best.
Thus, when our children make their choice,
We should trust nature, and rejoice.

WEDDING JITTERS

This poem has its origins in 1990, when I was the father of the bride at the wedding of our oldest daughter, Julie. I found it reassuring later, first when Ian got married in 2005, and then in 2010 at the wedding of our youngest daughter, Rebecca. It is immediately and wholly accessible, but is designed to surprise by refocussing the expectations that would usually be aroused by the title.

JAMES THE FIRST

Your mother looks at you with eyes that speak
Devotion without bounds. Two tiny feet
Curl downwards, outwards, inwards and then meet,
Move out again, and stretch as if to seek
New freedoms from the womb. You scratch your cheek,
And spatter debris over clothes and seat,
When, like a fledgling, you strain up to eat,
And flap your wings below your hungry beak.
How can it be, that helpless and so small,
You've come to dominate with your demands,
To have us always at your beck and call,
Competing to fulfil your least commands?
Dear Grandson James, now King above us all,
Love rules this concourse of your subject hands.

JAMES THE FIRST

J ames Michael was born to our eldest daughter, Julie, and
her husband, Andrew, on 27/7/96, and was our first
grandchild. This poem was written when he was about
eighteen months old. The contents speak for themselves, and
it will be seen that the use of a number in the title ('the First')
prepares the way for the use of 'demands' in line 10,
'commands' in line 12, and 'King' and 'rules' in the
concluding couplet. This is a Petrarchan sonnet, and is the
first of four sonnets which are included in this work. What,
then, is a Petrarchan sonnet?

Early sonnets are thought to have originated in Italy in
the thirteenth century as relatively short love poems, and later
and more defined examples on the Italian model are called
after Petrarch, one of the first Italian poets to write in the
vernacular. Various English writers adopted the form, but the
most important variant is known as the English or
Shakespearean Sonnet, and it is believed that this was
developed principally because of the difficulties involved in
the rhyme scheme of the original.

In the Petrarchan sonnet, there is a complete unity
between content and form, both of which have a distinct
predetermined and complementary development. While
beginning as a love poem, it soon became a medium for the
expression of other emotions as well as for profound thought
and deep beliefs. Content was developed in two stages to

match the division of the fourteen lines of the poem into an octave (eight lines) and a sestet (six lines) which were separated by a pause or break: thus, the octave was used to introduce and provide the initial development of an emotion, theme, thought or proposition, while the sestet then either provided further development or introduced a different perspective on the material, and allowed the poet to close by encapsulating the overall viewpoint or 'message' of the poem. The overarching unity between content and form was cemented by the use of a common line of measured syllables, the iambic pentameter and its variations, and unity within the octave and the sestet themselves was maintained by subdivisions using discrete rhyme schemes which produced two quatrains in the former and two tercets in the latter. The octave used a rhyme scheme which had only two full rhymes: thus, the first two quatrains had an identical rhyming pattern which may be expressed as A, B, B, A-A, B, B, A. The break or 'turn' into the sestet was signalled by a change in this rhyme scheme: the poet continued with the tercets and introduced two or three new rhymes, the most common formats being C, D, C, D, C, D, or C, D, E, C, D, E. Sometimes the sestet was subdivided into another quatrain followed by a rhyming couplet thus giving C, D, C, D, E, E. It can be seen that these Italian models would never have more than five full rhymes, and that the octave and the sestet should be genuine stanzas, marked by the use of punctuation which preserves their integrity and prevents devices like enjambment which would disrupt the 'turn' and impair the symmetry of the poem as a whole.

Shakespeare has been credited with 154 sonnets, and he has given his name to the English version, though others were using it before him. It differs from the Petrarchan in form rather than in content, and this is sometimes acknowledged by presenting it as three quatrains followed by a couplet rather than as a block. The major advantage it has over its rival lies in the rhyme scheme, which only requires seven rhyming words as in A, B, A, B – C, D, C, D – E, F, E, F – G, G. There have been some variations on this pattern, mainly by reverting to the rhyme order of the older version, thus giving, for example, A, B, B, A – C, D, D, C – E, F, F, E – G, G, and other permutations. They are all easier to write than the true Petrarchan sonnet since they do not require two words that have four rhymes which must still be the 'right words' from a sense point of view. This is one reason why it is the pure form of the Italian version that has come to be regarded by many as the highest expression of the art of the poet.

Many of the poems which are today offered as 'sonnets' have little in common with either the Italian or English models. The most alarming fault is the failure to preserve the essential unity in the overall development of content related to form. Some can't manage to keep to fourteen lines, which forces one to ask how many lines would be needed either below or above fourteen for the word sonnet to become inapplicable, and why this new number should be chosen rather than any other. Some apparently can't manage fourteen pentameters in a row, or cope with the predetermined rhyme scheme(s). Others deliberately destroy the 'turn' between the octave and the sestet by inappropriate enjambment(s), and yet others use slant rhymes improperly, seemingly failing to understand that such rhymes can draw attention to themselves and can thereby impair the sense rhythm which should be shown by the punctuation at the end of a sentence. Ruth Padel, in *52 Ways of Looking at a Poem* (Chatto and Windus, 2002), argues that modern sonnets 'challenge' and 'play with' traditional sonnet 'rules', and that what they keep is 'the feel or spirit of the sonnet as a kind of concentratedly reflective poetic box'. It seems to me that such offerings bear about as much relation to true sonnets as 'bastard' feudalism bore to feudalism proper, and that cynics might argue that many are the outcome of failed attempts to write in the traditional way, so that 'playing with the rules' is a rationalisation after the event. This particular 'poetic box', like Pandora's box in Classical mythology, should be kept firmly shut. For an object lesson in how to apply accepted rudiments of criticism to a Petrarchan sonnet, please see Alison Chisholm's analysis of my own prizewinning poem, *A Sonnet for my Still-born Brother*.

JAMES THE SECOND

A second James over our family reigns.
Like all our babes, he loves to eat and sleep,
While doting parents round their home must creep,
Embracing without rancour strains and pains
Which batter both their bodies and their brains.
And daily at his every whim they leap,
And then at night an anxious vigil keep,
While weight he gains, and normal life constrains.
Yet this addition to our kith and kin,
This little tyrant barely three months old,
Can show a beaming face that's free from sin,
And dares us human love to now withhold.
And, since we know forgiveness is love's twin,
We tell inquirers he's as good as gold.

JAMES THE SECOND

James Earl is the first grandson of my younger brother, Nigel, being born on 29/11/97 to his elder son, Martin, and his partner, Sharon. This is the second sonnet in these poems, and was written when James was about three months old.

In form, the poem is designed to pair with the previous one, presenting a standard octave and sestet with a clearly defined 'turn'. It is constructed from two enjambed quatrains followed by another quatrain and a couplet, and uses only four rhymes in total. Like the previous poem, this one is also rounded off with a two line conclusion which contains the 'message' of the poem.

The title follows on from 'James the First', and is reinforced by the words 'reigns' and 'tyrant' which harmonise with 'King' in the previous poem and find practical expression in the activities described in the octave.

A FISHY TALE

A little baby catfish went swimming with his mum,
And as he swam the mud he stirred, so he could fill his tum.
He burrowed and burrowed with his nose,
And a terrible, terrible odour arose.

Now, this little baby catfish saw that life's not fair,
And to his mum in fishy words his thoughts he did lay bare.
'Ohhh!' he wailed. 'My life is one long hell.
For every time I eat, I also make a smell.'

'My head is far too large, and my body far too stout,
And I've three pairs of whiskers which give me many a clout.
And, what's more, I suffer from a lack
Of hard protective spines, to guard my tender back.'

'My eyes are far too small, and my much too slimy skin
Seems not to want to do its job and hold my flat sides in.
And, what's worst of all – Ohhh! Woe is me!
Why am I plain old black? Why aren't I ebony?'

At this our little catfish began to cry and cry,
And as he cried he cursed his fate, and be resolved to die.
'I'll end it all,' he sobbed. 'Then I'll fly
To our Great Fish Goddess, who lives up in the sky.'

His mum could hardly listen, of him she was so fond,
And to his plaintive murmurings she gently did respond.

'Oh, no! Don't go! Please, please stay,' said she,
'Please stay while I explain how things are meant to be.'

'When I was much, much younger, my mum I did tell too
The sort of thoughts that seem today to come and trouble you.
So, listen, and you will hear from me
The things that my mum heard, at her own mother's knee.'

'We can't change the way we're born, so catfish we must be.
We're not to let more handsome fish excite our jealousy.
But we must strive – in God's Mistressplan –
To always knuckle down, and do the best we can.'

'We must live in deep, dark holes, and forage in the mud,
And we've been shaped to do that work in ways no others could.
And, though you find the smells so trying,
It's our cleaning stops the other fish from dying.'

'Now, listen. All fish have their part in the Great One's scheme,
And neither your form nor your colour are all that they seem.
Never, never feel that you're hated,
For the Great One herself loves all she's created.'

A little baby catfish went swimming with his mum,
And as he swam the mud he stirred, so he could fill his tum.
He laughed and laughed in his fishy way,
For he had the answers to what others might say.

A FISHY TALE

This originated as an aid to the socialisation of our two youngest children when Ian was about seven and Rebecca about five. The poem was written for them, and particularly for the former, at a time when they were beginning to experience life's rude knocks outside the family home. Hence, by implication, it stresses the importance of both parents and grandparents as sources of comfort, knowledge and wisdom.

Beginning with the title, the poem uses humour to lighten and to hide its more serious intentions, so that the form, structure, language and content should be evaluated on the basic principle of 'fitness for purpose'. It should be remembered that it is meant to be read aloud to small children, and to be accompanied by facial expressions and dramatic gestures. The occasional word (e.g. 'odour', 'plaintive', 'strive' and 'forage') may have to be explained. I make no apology for this, because the enlargement of vocabulary is a legitimate function of children's literature. Thus, if my memory serves me correctly, I learned the word 'oblivion' from A. G. Street's *Farmer's Glory* (a catapult was used to sweep a sparrow into oblivion from off a house roof) and 'mortified' from Mark Twain (either Huck or Tom claimed that he could not get out of bed because his big toe was mortified).

THE GHOST OF THE ANCIENT MARINER

The Man on Watch half-closed his eyes,
Then wide awake came he.
A hand had clutched his brawny arm –
Yet no flesh could he see.

'I know thee, Ancient Mariner,
I know those eyes so bright.
And I'll not fear, though you're so near,
And here appear at night.'

'While wedding guest you stopped me once
A tortured tale to tell.
You slew a trusting albatross –
A curse then on you fell.'

'But I your penance, too, did hear,
And took you at your word.
My soul I've saved by loving God,
And man, and beast, and bird.'

'Why come you now to trouble me,
When you should be at rest?'
The ghost here dropped his hand, and cried,
'Oh! That I too were blessed.'

'Would that I could be blessed,' he cried,
'But it's too late for me.
For penance new I must yet do,
For all eternity.'

'From shore a cabin-boy I saw,
And sensed his awful need.
So I embarked to reap his heart.
Oh! Irony, indeed!'

'Soon sailed we to the Southern Seas,
With squalls and swells sure sown,
And soon our ship shook to her seams,
And split, and sank like stone.'

'None save two souls survived the storm,
And on one raft were found.
And day by day, and night by night,
Were to each other bound.'

'Then food ran out, and water, too,
And pain came cold on pain.
And one did trip and lose his grip,
And never rose again.'

'For blood did drip down from his lip,
As warm as any wine;
And flesh did slip from off his hip,
As sweet as any swine.'

'A cut! A cut! A smooth, smooth, cut!
A cut as fine can be.
A slice of choicest boyish flesh –
And, through death, life for me.'

'I saw a sail and cleaned my knife
While balanced on one knee.
An albatross, swooping across,
Swept me into the sea.'

'Sharks snatched their fill: soon all was still.
My soul to judgement sped,
Where heaven's bliss was barred to me
By sins best left unsaid.'

'Instead, ahead, the dread undead
Wait now to walk with me.
And penance new I must yet do
For all eternity.'

THE GHOST OF THE ANCIENT MARINER

This is a nonsense poem whose title came from a competition set by *Writing Magazine*, which imposed a limit of sixty lines. The whole concept is problematic as Coleridge states that the life of the Mariner after his voyage was already one long penance, formalised at 'uncertain' intervals by the recurrence of a 'woeful agony' which forced him to wander from 'land to land' until he intuitively recognised someone who was in dire need of the moral found in his tale, and to whom he had to recount it in order that his own pain should be assuaged. The moral is found in the following lines: 'He prayeth well, who loveth well Both man, and bird and beast.' I had never written a ballad, and hence this, together with solving the problem of how the Mariner could possibly become a ghost, and amusing my family, were the main determinants of the poem.

Coleridge's *Rime* is a ballad, a term which is similar to the word sonnet in that it encapsulates both content and form. A genuine ballad is always a narrative: it tells a story which will eventually conclude with a resolution to which a moral is often attached. English ballads use the quatrain as their basic unit, and there is no upper or lower limit to the number of stanzas, though very few have less than seven. Ballads are usually subdivided into three types: the common metre, the long metre, and the short metre. All use either octosyllabic or hexasyllabic lines, the former having four stressed syllables and the latter, three. The common metre, as its name implies, is the most used, counts 8, 6, 8, 6, and has a rhyme scheme of A, B, C, B. The short metre, counting 6, 6, 8, 6, generally has a similar cross rhyming scheme, whereas the long metre counts 8, 8, 8, 8, and most commonly has a full rhyming scheme, either A, B, A, B, or A, A, B, B. However, as most ballads historically were orally transmitted and were often sung and/or danced to, many contain deviations from these ideal patterns, and legitimately include extra unstressed and half-stressed syllables, inversions, archaisms, repetitions, nonsense words and phrases, and the subversion of the quatrain through the addition of one or two line refrains.

I have followed Coleridge in using the rhythm and rhyme scheme of the traditional common metre ballad. However, the length of his poem allows variations in both stanza length and rhyme scheme, whereas the need to drive the narrative forward meant that I had to keep strictly to the standard form and to avoid unnecessary refrains and repetitions. Excepting these, I have incorporated all other techniques appropriate to ballads. Thus, I have kept the language simple and direct, and have used inversion, internal and end rhyme, alliteration, assonance and consonance to support the rhythm.

Coleridge was a wonderful poet. He had an instinctive sense of rhythm and was equally proficient in his choice of language and in his construction of stanzas. I have previously referred to my rural childhood in Lincolnshire and my fear of going out alone at night in the dark, and in Book Two of this work I raise the question of the relative merits of writing in prose or verse. This stanza from the *Ancient Mariner* could not be bettered in prose, and I cannot read it without an involuntary raising of the hairs on the back of my neck.

> Like one that on a lonesome road
> Doth walk in fear and dread,
> And having once turn'd round, walks on,
> And turns no more his head;
> Because he knows a frightful fiend
> Doth close behind him tread.

IS THIS THE FACE?

When, as I'm shaving, I caress my face,
I think of time gone by.
I feel my years
As blades discover ancient scars,
And trace the paths of once-important tears.

I strain through glasses I am forced to wear
If I'm to stay unscathed.
They hide my fears
That greying and receding hair
Gives early warning baldness nears.

I run the razor up my scrawny neck
Towards my chin and mouth.
My false teeth shine,
Lying between two sallow cheeks,
And lying in the pretence that they're mine.

Truth's in crows' feet which corner time-worn eyes,
And in the furrows on my brow.
It hides in soap,
Until, exposed with trembling stroke,
It shouts my aging image – and I mope.

IS THIS THE FACE?

I still possess a by-election leaflet from 1977 which includes a flattering photograph of myself taken when I was seemingly in my prime, and about twenty years later this triggered the original idea for this poem. It is a fiction in that it is concerned exclusively with the physical manifestations of aging, and deliberately excludes any of the compensations arising from the same process. The title was used to begin sentences in plays by both Shakespeare and Marlowe. As line 4 indicates, I now use two-bladed disposable razors.

COGITO, ERGO SUM

'I THINK, THEREFORE I AM.'

'Cogito, ergo sum.' Oh, what a thought!
It makes my blood run faster than it ought,
And, by distending arteries and veins,
It aggravates my throbbing head
With arm and chest and other pains.

'Cogito, ergo sum'. Now I'm much worse.
I never should have penned the previous verse.
Descartes has signalled what I always missed.
I was busy, busy living,
And just assumed that I exist.

'Cogito, ergo sum.' I'm sinking fast,
But comfort find in Descartes at my last.
For if I have no actuality,
Then undertakers should agree…
To waive their fee…
And bury me…
For free… Eeee!

COGITO, ERGO SUM

'I THINK, THEREFORE I AM.'

The title of this nonsense poem is taken from Descartes' *Second Meditation*, 1637. The proposition and its conclusion have become much loved by philosophers, and they have used it to torture themselves and others for well over three and a half centuries. My poem is hence dedicated to all those who have sat in tutorials brainstorming on vital questions like whether their teachers exist; whether mathematics is true; or whether we can trust our senses.

PART TWO

POEMS FOR PAIN

POEMS FOR PAIN

REMEMBERING THE FEW

At my nativity, those lovely skies
Hymned by our poets who in them rainbows saw,
Had been turned dark, and made a battleground
By one who chose to slip his dogs of war.

But in those dreadful days around my birth
Our airmen rose, and skills and youth supplied.
And they restored those skies our poets sing,
Though in that cleansing, many of them died.

Churchill himself defined their epitaph
In one sad sentence which we quote today.
Their early deaths by gun and crash and fire
Meant we survived to work and rest and play.

Honour these dead by loving life, and guard
Your freedoms which their sacrifice secured.
And when aggressors hunt again, stand fast:
Only through pain is lasting peace procured.

REMEMBERING THE FEW

I was born on August 16th, 1940, at the height of what is now called 'The Battle of Britain', and this poem is my tribute to the men and women who took part in that struggle for air supremacy. 'Never in the field of human conflict', stated Churchill, 'was so much owed by so many to so few', for if the outcome had been different, then in all probability Britain would have come under Nazi occupation.

Millions were to die or be cruelly maimed before the war was over, and most of these were civilians. Our family was lucky in that my father and his two brothers eventually emerged unscathed from active service, and our losses were limited to bomb damage to property. But many people were not so fortunate, and I believe that we should publicly commemorate our dead, and should offer emotional and financial support to those whose lives are still impoverished by past and present conflicts. Those who do not share this view should familiarise themselves with the details of the Nazi blueprints for a conquered Britain, and with the too real horrors suffered in countries in occupied Europe and elsewhere.

THE ATOM BOMBS AND US

'He'll be back when the war is over,'
Is what we were always told.
But the war in Europe drew to a close,
And promises made us bold.

'I'll be back once the war is over.'
We had learned this off by heart.
For he'd never have time to play with us,
But would kiss, and soon depart.

'He'll be back now the war is over,
And this time he'll stay, you'll see.
We've done for the Japs with new-fangled bombs.
Now, shut up, and eat your tea!'

THE ATOM BOMBS AND US

This poem is written from the perspective of a mother and her children who were caught up in events which they would never have instigated, about which they had little knowledge, and over which they had no control. They see developments solely in terms of how they and their loved ones will be affected, and have no conception of any wider implications. My older brother, David, was born on November 2nd, 1938, before the war began, and Nigel arrived on March 7th, 1944, while it was still on. Dad was called up for September 6th, 1941, and released on December 15th, 1945. Thus, Dave and I had spent over four years of our most formative period without any real knowledge of our father, though this does not seem to have done us any harm.

I am aware that many people today will raise an eyebrow at the wording and content of line 11, and that there are those who may find it offensive. However, this poem is not written with the benefit of either hindsight or rose-coloured spectacles, nor with a view to being politically correct. It represents a genuine and instantaneous response to an event whose long-term significance in terms of human suffering or international politics was only dimly perceived, if it was perceived at all.

When I was young, I never knew anyone who agonised over the Allied use of atomic weapons, and my own knowledge of the Japanese came mainly from the material that was available at the former P.O.W. exhibitions which we visited when at the seaside. I was about sixteen when I first realised that there were people who regarded the use of atomic weapons as a war crime, and about eighteen when I realised that some of these people had their own agendas. Whatever their motivations, I believe that they miss the point. The compelling responsibility of Allied governments was to our own servicemen and civilians, and the consensus of modern research is that the bombs hastened the surrender of Japan. The actual deaths and suffering through the use of atomic bombs at Hiroshima and Nagasaki have therefore to be balanced against the potential losses in both combatant and non-combatant Japanese, Allied and neutral lives through a continuation of conventional warfare. There is no doubt that the casualties arising from the last would have been considerably greater.

A SONNET FOR MY STILL-BORN BROTHER

You slept, and moved, and kicked within the womb,
Making us guess those parts we could not see;
And we, touching and prodding tenderly,
Saw the skin ripple as you sought more room.
And each new day you strove towards your doom,
While we watched on, and wondered what you'd be
As rites of passage followed infancy,
And our support ensured that you would bloom.
But your life-giving then denying cord
Strangled our hopes and fears without a sound,
And left us tears to wet a scythe-cut sward,
Your unnamed and unconsecrated ground.
    Nature decrees some innocents must die,
    And those who love them will be made to cry.

A SONNET FOR MY STILL-BORN BROTHER

This is the third sonnet in this collection and, like its predecessors, it takes the Petrarchan form. However, it changes the rhyme scheme of the sestet from C, D, C, D, C, D to a discrete rhyming quatrain, C, D, C, D, followed by a discrete rhyming couplet, E, E. I have already referred to this sonnet in my Author's Preface: an earlier version won one of the competitions offered by *Writing Magazine* and was featured with a detailed critique in their Annual Competitions Guide for 2006-7.

The original poem read as follows:

A MESSAGE FOR MY STILL-BORN BROTHER

You slept, and moved, and kicked within the womb
Making us guess those parts we could not see;
And we, touching and prodding tenderly,
Saw the skin ripple as you sought more room.
And every day you strove towards your doom,
While we watched on, and wondered what you'd be
As rites-of-passage followed infancy,
And our support ensured that you would bloom.
But your life-giving then denying cord
Strangled our hopes and fears without a sound,

And left us tears to wet a scythe-cut sward,
Your unnamed and unconsecrated ground.
Rest sure our faith stays vested in our Lord,
And in that mercy you've already found.

Alison Chisholm's analysis covered all the usual ways in which a sonnet should be appraised, but was positive in every respect. The poem was 'powerful' and 'intensely moving' without ever becoming 'sentimental', and embraced dramatic irony in contrasting the hopes of the opening octet with the tragic outcome involved in the sestet. She accepted the legitimacy of a further 'turn' in the final two lines, where a positive assertion of religious faith and belief in the afterlife concludes the account. She liked the simplicity of the language, particularly the use of monosyllables, and the images involved in 'touching and prodding' and in 'seeing the skin ripple as you sought more room'. She thought that 'sward' might seem archaic but was 'exactly right in this context – proof that a spectacular exception can prove a rule'. She believed 'scythe-cut', with its double image of neatly controlled grass and the 'grim reaper', was especially effective. She found no wasted words, and picked out two 'highly memorable phrases' in 'As rites-of-passage followed infancy' and in 'your life-giving then denying cord/Strangled our hopes'. She was happy that all rhyming words had been correctly chosen yet had also maintained the sense and syntax of the poem. And, lastly, with respect to the metre, she noted that variety had been added to the customary iambic pentameters by the introduction of three initial trochaic substitutions, where the opening iambus is reversed giving a stressed syllable followed by an unstressed, and then continuing with the expected additional four feet of unstressed followed by stressed syllables.

Despite the professionalism of Alison's appraisal, I was never 100% happy with this sonnet, and struggled for six years to improve it. As a result, the final version differs from the original in three ways, two involving content and one involving scansion. Both the title and the concluding couplet of the original were addressed to the still-born baby and involved religious beliefs which reflected my upbringing: hence, the easiest changes were to these, and they are now written to have a universal application and hence, hopefully, a universal appeal. The change involving scansion was far harder to pinpoint: my poet's ear insisted that something was wrong, but I could not find it. Eventually, I realised that I was reading line five as having ten syllables whereas in fact it had eleven – the original line began 'and every day' (five syllables) but I was reading it as 'and ev'ry day' (four syllables). At first I wondered whether I should bother to change it, but one day out of the blue the solution came, and the new line now not only scans correctly but also has added nuance in its meaning.

In the early 1960s my mother was given a small bound volume with the title *The Longfellow Birthday Book*. Measuring about three inches across and about four inches down, this lovely work takes the form of a diary. When open, the left-hand pages contain three dates followed by one or sometimes more quotations from Longfellow. The right-hand pages were formerly blank, and on them birthdays and other things to be remembered could be recorded. One page contains the dates 13th-15th December; and opposite December 14th, and as the only entry on the page, my mother wrote: 'Baby boy died, 1949'.

That baby would have been her fourth, and she would have quickly got over her disappointment that it was yet another boy. A few months previously my parents had moved into a brand new house, and both the baby and Mum's own birthday were due just before our first Christmas there. It was thus to have been such a joyful time. However, things did not go as planned, and although I was only nine years old, I have never forgotten the events of the day that my mother has pinpointed.

My brothers had both been farmed out to relatives or friends for the week of the birth, while for reasons unknown to me I had been retained at home. I had been warned what to expect. Soon after teatime the unwelcome noises coming from upstairs stopped, and there was a strange silence broken occasionally by muted voices or whisperings. Eventually, I recognised the heavy tread of my father walking across the upstairs floor and landing, and then coming down the stairs. I rose from the table where I was playing cards, and opened the living-room door to greet him. Ashen-faced, he came slowly down the stairs, and without a word he pushed me back into the living-room and closed the door. I heard him go outside, and then I heard him apparently hammering. Soon he re-entered the house and I heard him go back upstairs. There were more whisperings, and then more hammerings, and then there were also more awful and different screams from my mother. Soon I heard my father again coming down the stairs, and by now thoroughly frightened, I crept to the living-room door and re-opened it. I saw my father slowly feeling his way down the treads, his head slightly angled as he looked down at where he was placing his feet. His face was more white and even grimmer than before, and he was carrying a large wooden box. I recognised this immediately as one of the crates that we kept in the shed for the winter storage of vegetables. He had filled in the gaps in the sides, and seemed to have added a makeshift lid. He brushed past me and went through the kitchen and then out the back door to the shed. Some time later he came back into the house and into the living-room, re-opening the door that I had re-closed. He said that the baby had died; that it was past my bedtime; that I would have to get ready myself; that I couldn't see Mum until tomorrow; and that I would find out everything then. Mum was all right, and I wasn't to worry.

Subsequently, the baby was buried in unconsecrated ground within our local churchyard, and my mother would periodically rediscover the grave and attempt to neaten it up with a pair of large scissors. Since her death the exact location of the grave is unknown to the family.

It can be seen that the substance of the poem is to be taken quite literally.

FOR THE CARERS OF CHILDREN UNDERGOING MAJOR OPERATIONS

We see a trust which wounds flow from their eyes,
And feel it whirl within our hearts.
We know that our response will be in lies –
White lies we'll hide through fits and starts.

We watch half-smiles of doubt begin to die
As words to warm and soothe take hold.
We wince, but overwhelm and pacify.
We push away the truth, untold.

We show no guilt as farewell hugs we give.
We're worrying at the words of men
Who weigh the odds by which our children live,
And warn in terms of 'if' and 'then'.

We use our hugs to hide and wipe our tears
Which newly squeeze from ducts thought dry.
We still dissemble though the crisis nears,
And will that they won't see us cry.

We kiss goodbye as they're wheeled to their fate,
And straighten till they're out of sight.
We slowly walk to where we're told to wait.
And there we pray, as well we might.

We're wearied by a wily inner voice,
Whisp'ring betrayal of a child
When we pre-empt its clear and conscious choice,
And leave it blinkered and beguiled.

We quiet such thoughts that on self-hatred thrive,
And re-affirm that we are right.
We've said those things which keep our child alive:
Truth's not our ally in that fight.

And so we wait, our early parts played out,
While others bring their skills to bear.
And, pensive in our pain, we have no doubt
We'll be absolved by all who care.

FOR THE CARERS OF CHILDREN UNDERGOING MAJOR OPERATIONS

The idea for this poem came from two television programmes broadcast on consecutive nights. Both contained human interest stories in which children faced life-threatening situations and parents took agonising decisions. The poem attempts to marry a narrative of two fairly common experiences (parents waiting, firstly, by the bedside of a conscious child in advance of a major operation, and secondly, in the waiting-room until it is over) with the thoughts and feelings of the parents who are involved. Initially, mainly because of the combination of narrative and reflection, I decided to use iambic pentameters for the whole poem. However, once the eight verses had been decided on, I found that thirty-two lines of iambic pentameter tended to overshadow the meaning, and thus destroyed the point of the exercise. Eventually, I settled on two pentameters and two tetrameters in the combination 10, 8, 10, 8, and also on a closed pattern rhyming scheme of A, B, A, B, to be applied consistently throughout.

It is now accepted that there is an unexplained affinity between the functioning of the mind and of the body. My poem defends parents who try to take advantage of that affinity, even if it involves them in a degree of deception. Nevertheless, every case must take into account the age and maturity of the child concerned, and hence must be considered on its own individual merits.

REFLECTIONS ON THE DEATH OF A DAUGHTER OF FRIENDS

If I had but known, that one day very soon
She would be lying white and still,
Machined,
Insensate,
Waiting to die,
And that her father by her bed would watch the hours
In whispering agony –
Then I would have been more kind to her
Than I sometimes was.

And, if I had but known, that through her drawn-out death
She would bring life and sight to others
Hospitalised,
Dependent,
Hoping for hope,
And that her mother would take comfort from those awful deeds
That were her wish –
Then I would have found more time for her
Than I sometimes did.

But if I had only known, when she was just a child
And hesitantly played around my knee
Expectant,
Vulnerable,
Full of life,

If I had known, only, that one day in a church I'd stand
Choking a reversed farewell –
Then I would have shown more love for her
Than I sometimes did.

REFLECTIONS ON THE DEATH
OF A DAUGHTER OF FRIENDS

Sara Louise Winson was born on February 18th, 1962, and died on October 21st, 1981. She was the second of five daughters, and had just begun her first term at Nottingham University when she received horrific injuries in a car accident. She never regained consciousness, and after a short time on life-support systems, her organs (including her heart) were taken for transplants in accordance with her known wishes.

People who had no personal knowledge of Sara, and people without children of their own, were profoundly moved by the circumstances surrounding her death. Our grief was greater, as her parents are among our oldest and closest friends, as we had watched her grow up, and as we are blessed with three daughters and one son. Yet our pain could hardly compare with that suffered by her immediate family, her parents and her sisters. Her death, unexpected and accidental, and before she could make a mature contribution, exemplified Chaucer's emphasis on 'Dame Fortune and her Treacherous Wheel'. It was an event which reversed the natural order of things, and which seems both meaningless and cruel.

My poem reflects my own coming to terms with the loss of Sara, and, by implication, of any of my own children. It should be read slowly and softly. It was written over a period of about six months, being completed in the summer of 1982. It would be pleasing to think that it could be a source of comfort and strength to others, and that in consequence some additional good might be fashioned out of the tragedy from which it emanated.

Since I wrote this, we have ourselves experienced what must be every parent's worst nightmare. In June 2006, our middle daughter, Victoria Jane, suffered an aortic dissection, and was subsequently shown to have been born with Marfan Syndrome, a spontaneous mutation affecting her connective tissues. She died on January 28th, 2009, aged 39 years. Our position differed from that of Sara's parents in that the National Health Service was able to give us an extra two and a half years with Vicky, and she had worked long enough as a psychiatric nurse and stress counsellor to be able to make a very valued contribution to the sum total of human happiness. Further, she had been strongly religious from her childhood, and this helped us all to come to terms with what my wife and I knew from 2007 would be the inevitable outcome.

ACCEPTING THE DEATH OF CHILDREN

As we nurture and love our children,
We say that they're 'Heaven-sent',
And we forget we can't know God's purpose,
And that a child is only lent.
But when from our arms they're so cruelly wrested,
And we then by this are so cruelly tested,
We shall know that the love which we thought was spent
Forms the sole seed-corn of the whole firmament.
Loving, Accepting: these are God's will,
And beloveds, though gone, yet stay for us still.

ACCEPTING THE DEATH
OF CHILDREN

Originally, a verse similar to this was to have formed the concluding part of the previous poem, which had been provisionally titled 'Acceptance'. However, external criticism eventually convinced me that I had produced a mismatch in both form and content. With respect to the form, the deliberate changes in line length and rhythm produced a discordant effect rather than the harmony I was looking for, particularly as it also introduced a rhyming scheme. With respect to content, the introduction of a religious element jarred with the secular nature of the first three stanzas. I therefore decided that the previous poem should be presented as it now is.

However, our experiences with Vicky and her friends taught me that in general those who believe in an afterlife are able to bear any sort of bereavement with more equanimity than those who have no such beliefs. It was one of our former vicars, the Rev. Maurice Green, who reminded me, in the context of Sara's death, that our children are only lent to us. Mindful of this, I have made what would have been the concluding verse into a self-contained poem, and it is written for those who believe in angels, as our Vicky did while she was alive.

SENILE DEMENTIA

Her eyes were nearly brown,
Though flecks of black and green
Which beautified her irises
Could readily be seen.
And while she thrived, if she became elated,
Her eyes would flash as the colours animated.

But as her illness firmed,
And memory declined,
Her eyes gave up their sparks, and in
A dormant state reclined.
Yet, cruelly, at times she seemed all too aware,
And asked – and asked – and asked – why she was living
    there.

And when at last she died,
And I sat by her bed,
I stretched my hand and closed those eyes
Which now were doubly dead.
And just one tear my own eyes failed to smother,
As I knelt down by the body of my mother.

SENILE DEMENTIA

These words are officially recorded on my mother's death certificate. Widowed in 1974, she returned to her native Lincoln in 1981, but in about 1983 she began to experience minor strokes and/or epileptic fits as a result of which she could not be allowed to retain her independence. Subsequently, she lived with us for a short while, until her condition became such that we were forced to transfer her to a private residential home.

The earliest symptoms displayed by my mother were very similar to those now generally associated with Alzheimer's disease. She became increasingly confused and disorientated, and it was soon obvious that she was losing her short-term memory. She was not, however, 'demented' as this is popularly understood. One of the worst features of the early stages of her illness was that she seemed to know what was happening to her, and this in itself caused her further and great distress. Thus, she would observe that she had lived too long. She would ask if she was going mad. And she would plead with me not to allow her to be 'put in the loony bin', as her early upbringing would have it. On the other hand, she would occasionally regress to the Second World War and to other times when her father was alive, and she would attempt to make sense of new situations by drawing on memories she already possessed. For example, whenever her brother Harold phoned the Home she would tell him that she was playing bowls at Skegness, and would be coming home tomorrow. (Harold had been winning trophies at Skegness since his twenties, and from the 1960s Mum herself had taken up bowls. She started with two local teams, and eventually played for Lincolnshire Ladies and at Skegness during 'Bowls Week'.)

I do not know if it is possible to accurately convey the emotions of those who care for and try to cope with people who suffer as my mother had to suffer. You watch someone who once possessed rare talents like playing the piano by ear and taking shorthand at 140 words a minute, who believed that life should be enjoyed to the full, and who had often been described as the life and soul of the party degenerate in less than four years into someone who could not fully control her bodily functions, and whose good waking moments were spent in a state of bewilderment and bad ones in states that varied from mild panic to abject terror. You have to stop taking your children on visits, since, not being recognised, their nearness to you merely causes more distress. You cannot converse in a meaningful way: any conversation is like treading in a minefield where defined markers had once existed but have been haphazardly altered. When you visit, you begin to do so with a heavy heart. Though, on arrival, you may be recognised and trusted, as I always was, you know that immediately you are out of sight your visit will have been forgotten, and that anything you have said will have gone in one ear and out of the other. And you have to prepare yourself for shocks, like the one I received when Mum failed for the first time to recognise Dad in photographs.

Both my brothers were clearly moved by the first draft of this poem, Nigel declaring in a quiet voice that he believed it had 'said it all'. I hope it will accord with the feelings of others who have experienced circumstances similar to these, and will also be accessible to those who lack direct knowledge of this illness and have to rely on hearsay for their information.

WELCOME MY NIGHT

I would lie still, in silent solitude,
Whilst creeping night snuffed out the light,
And brought a new beatitude.

Eyes closed, I'd stay awake, and contemplate
Our Mother Earth before my birth,
Before my own pathetic fate.

I'd tell myself I don't need to be brave
If I am burned, or ground is turned,
For only ashes seek a grave.

I'd welcome sure relief from nursing chores
My body breeds as aging speeds,
And which my conscious mind abhors.

And welcome, too, the final end of pains
Which escalate, and enervate,
And generate their own refrains.

And I'd discount the loss my loves would feel,
For though they'd grieve if I should leave,
Their hurt is one that time will heal.

So let me lie in silent solitude.
Let soothing night snuff out the light,
While I fade out with gratitude.

WELCOME MY NIGHT

Some readers may be familiar with 'Do not go gentle into that good night' by Dylan Thomas, which can be found in *The New Oxford Book of English Verse* (1972), p. 942. His poem is a villanelle, and I have never liked either that form or his particular content. The form can lead to the occasional memorable line, but I feel that on the whole it is not worth the time and effort that has to be put into composing it.

My own poem retains the characteristic pentameters and three line stanzas but increases their number from six to seven while dispensing with the fourth line of the last one and with the repetition of whole lines. I have used rhymes to link lines one and three, and a fixed caesura and full internal rhymes to balance the second line of each verse. The partial repetition in the first and last verses is used to unify the whole poem and to reinforce what it is saying.

This poem is written for my mother and the millions like her for whom death is a welcome release.

YOUR FATHER'S LAST WISH

During that doleful time after I've died,
And you're made pale by grief and lack of sleep,
You'll find that I have left you fortified
By that same love which causes you to weep.
And ever in your heart this love you'll keep.
And ever it will comfort and will guide
When tribulations make your road more steep,
And I can be no longer by your side.
Then you will hear me shout out from my grave
That I was blessed four times as you were born,
And there was nothing further I could crave,
Nor any losses which I'd so much mourn.

    Thus, as your father loved you in times past,
    Let love, your first cause, also be your last.

YOUR FATHER'S LAST WISH

This sonnet was about twenty years in its making. In about 1985 I decided that I would like to leave a poem specifically for my children to remember me by, and in about 1990 I further decided that it would have to be a sonnet. In about 1995 I concluded that it was right to make it about love, but it should be addressed to our children collectively rather than incorporating them individually. In 2003 I abandoned the pure forms of the Petrarchan and Shakespearean sonnets in favour of a hybrid.

The octave retains the two rhymes of the Italian version, but uses the English pattern for the first quatrain, which it then reverses for the second, thus giving A, B, A, B – B, A, B, A as the new format. The integrity of the octave is thus preserved, and this allows a definite 'turn' into the sestet. This is then continued with the quatrain of C, D, C, D, common to both the English and Italian versions, and the sonnet is then finished with a rhyming couplet, E, E, giving a total of five rhymes as in the Italian version. The content is self-explanatory, though it should be noted that the word 'cause' in the last line carries two distinct meanings.

Vicky had studied English up to A Level. She had a great respect for poetry, and I am now very pleased that I was able to finish this and give her a copy in 2004, two years before she suffered her aortic dissection.

POEMS FOR PROFIT

A PRE-MODERNIST RATIONALE

(A) OVERVIEW

I stated in the Preface that many who agree with the views of Aristotle and Wordsworth which I then quoted would accept my long poems as verse but would deny that they were poetry. I also stated that all poems should be constructed on the general principle of 'fitness for purpose'. This Introduction to Book Two will involve discussions of the meaning and significance of the word 'poetry' and of 'fitness for purpose' as applied particularly to the contents and forms of my two long poems. However, as I also stated in the Preface, it is unnecessary to study this appreciation before reading the poems themselves. My description of these poems as 'long poems' is a relative concept only, being meaningful in comparison with my previous shorter efforts. They pale into insignificance when put beside the longer works of writers like Tennyson or Milton, or the *Cursor Mundi* of the early fourteenth century, a vernacular rhymed poem which (according to A. R. Myers) covered the history of the world from creation to Doomsday and took nearly 30,000 lines to do so.[1]

(B) ARISTOTLE AND THE MEANING OF POETRY

The development of a literary culture meant that authors soon had a choice between two differing forms of written communication. They could organise the sounds and stresses found within spoken words and exclamations, and hence within the sentences through which meaning is expressed, into either prose or verse, the most important difference between them being in the nature of the rhythms that were inherent in each. At some stage things that were written down as verse were given the general name of poetry, and it can be shown that this use of the word started very early and continued very late. Thus, in the fourth century B.C., Aristotle complained that his contemporaries described anything that was put into metrical form as poetry and, much later, Wordsworth could variously use the terms 'metrical arrangements', 'metrical language', 'metrical composition', 'writing in verse' and 'writing in metre' as synonyms for the same word or process.

If it is accepted that Aristotle was correct in his assertion concerning the custom of his contemporaries, then the original definition of poetry both distinguished it from prose and entailed the idea of metrical language. However, while this indicates that all verse could be described as poetry, it does not tell us whether everything could be put into verse, or whether, either by proscription or convention, poetry and prose were each reserved for particular areas or subjects to the exclusion of the other. It thus leaves open the question of whether the word 'poetry' embraced hidden meanings additional to the one already stated. Theoretically, prose and poetry as terms denoting forms of written communication might carry meanings not just with respect to their rhythms, but also with respect to their content (defined as the substance of the material, situations, values or emotions to be communicated) and to the status of that content as a form of knowledge (defined as the truth, validity or contemporary acceptability of that content). However, the Greeks could combine their enjoyment of verse with history (e.g. Homer's *Iliad* and *Odyssey*); with farming and the virtues of rural life (e.g. Hesiod's *Works and Days*); and with law and public administration (e.g. through the poems of Solon). Similarly, the Romans could learn their philosophy from Lucretius (*On the Nature of Things*); their agriculture and history from Virgil (the *Georgics* and the *Aeneid*); and their metres from Horace (*The Art of Poetry*). These examples show that Classical authors often chose their medium independently of their views on the truthfulness or utility of their contributions, so that they bequeathed works in verse the contents of which today would in all probability be put into prose. It thus appears that neither the word 'poetry' nor the word 'prose' could have carried any proscriptive meanings with respect to either their content or their veracity.

Further evidence points in the same direction. As authors moved from recording poetry and songs that were already extant and common property to composing poems of their own, and as literary criticism itself developed, it became necessary to devise category words with respect to content and/or form which would indicate features not entailed by the word poetry in itself. Classical civilisation thus produced works which have become known as epic or heroic poetry, didactic poetry, satiric poetry, and lyric poetry, with elegies and odes being regarded as offshoots of the last. These labels are thought necessary because they add to the basic definition of writing in metre, signifying principally the nature of the content to be anticipated, and sometimes the particular metre in which that content will be versified. But authors have various methods through which they can acquire their content: it can be a product of their own experience, imagination, or reasoning processes (i.e. intuition, introspection, fantasy, deduction or induction), or it may be obtained second hand, through copying, translation, hearsay and oral traditions. Hence, category words may also signify the stance adopted by the author and, by implication, may also hint at a claimed status as primarily fact or primarily fiction. An epic or heroic poem based on oral tradition may be thought to be less reliable than a didactic poem which incorporates an empirically-derived content. The signification, though, does not arise from the word 'poem', and this again shows that the terms prose and poetry related to the form of the communication and not to the material being communicated or to its status as a form of knowledge.

Enough has now been adduced to allow a critical examination of the remarks that I previously quoted from Aristotle, and the following translation, copied from an essay titled *Is Poetry a Dying Art?*, first published by Edmund

Wilson in 1938, provides a brief summary of the kernel of his argument:

> 'We have no common name for a mime of Sophron or Xenarchus and a Socratic conversation; and we should still be without one even if the imitation in the two instances were in trimeters or elegiacs or some other kind of verse – though it is the way with people to tack on 'poet' to the name of a metre, and talk of elegiac poets and epic poets, thinking that they call them poets not by reason of the imitative nature of their work, but indiscriminately by reason of the metre they write in. Even if a theory of medicine or physical philosophy be put forth in a metrical form, it is usual to describe the writer in this way. Homer and Empedocles, however, have really nothing in common apart from their metre; so that, if the one is to be called a poet, the other should be termed a physicist rather than a poet.'[2]

The use of 'it is the way with people' and of 'it is usual' shows that Aristotle believed he was describing orthodox opinion, and that this equated anything written in verse metre with poetry. But the remainder of the passage shows that Aristotle thought his contemporaries were in error: basically, he argued that the essence of poetry lay in its status as a work of 'imitation' and that this criterion for discrimination meant that some verse could not be described as poetry. His comment on Empedocles is logically consistent with his view already quoted in my Preface, namely that Herodotus put into verse would still be history and not poetry.

Unfortunately, it is very difficult today to understand exactly what Aristotle meant by his use of the term 'imitation', and as it is this term which seems to have been responsible for so much later debate, it calls for a deeper scrutiny.

In 1961 Professor Cameron in *Poetry and Dialectic* defined 'the making of poetry' as 'the making of fictions', and claimed that 'this in part at least overlapped' with the meaning of 'mimesis', which had been used by Aristotle to signify 'the distinguishing characteristics of the poetic activity'.[3] Wilson interpreted it as 'the creative art which had for its medium both prose and verse'.[4] 'Mimesis' has come down to us today as a specialist term in the biological sciences, where it denotes 'mimicry', or the close external resemblance between one animal and another, or between one animal and a plant or inanimate object. In Ancient Greece the term was related to others which involved the idea of 'imitation' or 'representation' as opposed to actual or real, and was applied to a particular form of imitation, namely the act of miming, or the dramatic representation of scenes from actual life by action and gesture but without words. Aristotle's first sentence made it clear that he was applying the idea to both prose and poetry, but he made it equally clear that his own times had no word which he could use for this, and so he was forced to use the word poetry itself. What was therefore needed was the coining of a new 'labelling' word which would have for its meaning the idea that Aristotle was trying to convey, and would additionally apply to both forms of written communication.

Instead, Aristotle sought to change the then current meaning of 'poetry'. This could have been acceptable if he had stopped at adding a new meaning to the existing one and if the new meaning had been compatible with that already in use. But he ignored this limitation, and the consequences were bizarre. In the first place, his definition cut across the conventional distinction between prose rhythm and verse metre by introducing a quality which might be found in both. This meant that they would no longer be seen as the two basic categories of written communication. It also meant that poetry became a word which excluded much existing poetry (i.e. 'non-imitative verse') yet paradoxically included much prose (i.e. 'imitative prose'). In the second place, his definition introduced a new category of writing based on process rather than on form: it made poetry a particular kind of creative activity ('an imitative work' – 'a creative art' – 'the making of fictions') governed by what later ages called 'the fancy' or 'the imagination'. As such, it became a term for a highly subjective process, and carried implications for both content and the status of that content as a form of knowledge, two things I have already shown as irrelevant to the prevailing definition. The absurdity of Aristotle's position is demonstrated by his contention concerning Herodotus, this example of his supporting evidence being in fact the reverse of what he supposed. Herodotus wrote in prose and claimed that his work was an 'historia', the Greek word for 'inquiry' or 'research', and Aristotle classified him with Empedocles because of the perceived 'non-imitative' nature of their writings. It is not relevant that Herodotus has been subsequently dubbed 'The Father of Lies' as well as 'The Father of History', or that the views of Empedocles concerning the nature of matter have been discredited.[5] What is relevant is that these authors were accepted by their contemporaries as writing truth rather than fiction, yet it is not difficult to show that they have little in common besides their prose, since the writing of history, unlike the writing of physics, is by definition a fundamentally creative activity.

Every second of the past once had its own reality, and that reality recedes into the darkness with every succeeding second, leaving only a fraction of the evidence necessary for reconstructing it. This surviving evidence is always incomplete, and may be significantly unrepresentative; and further, if it is evidence that has been written or drawn (i.e. if it is part of the recorded past) then it will additionally contain elements of conscious (i.e. deliberate) and unconscious (i.e. involuntary) bias. The raw materials of the historian are therefore inherently the result of subjective processes, and to these will be added others of a similar nature, namely those that pertain to the historian as an individual human being and as a member of the age during which he or she is writing. Historians as individuals may be influenced subconsciously by personal beliefs and attitudes in the spheres of, for example, race, politics and religion. They may also reflect the preoccupations and problems of their times, as happened when early twentieth century historians gave more attention to the lives of the common people, and later ones raised the profile of topics like slavery or feminism. All events, situations or developments which concern the historian are unique and non-repeatable: they are the product of an unquantifiable number of variables, each of which may simultaneously operate as cause and effect. Historians cannot formulate any 'laws of history' of universal application or significance, nor can they make any predictions except in the most general and non-specific terms. The only 'objective past' is that which has already come and gone: the idea of 'objective history' is nothing more than a contradiction in terms, since all historians produce work of a subjective nature and, although their titles may sometimes be the same, their contents will always be different. Historians, therefore, do not recreate or reconstruct the whole past: the best that they can achieve, within the constraints already indicated, is to fashion a representation of selected parts or aspects of the one and only once-real past. It is this that they make available to their contemporaries, and it is through this that they marry the languages of the past and the present, so that the former is enabled to speak to us in its own words but also those of historians. History books contain elements of description, narration and analysis – but they are the outcome of empathy, imagination and reason, acting either with or upon each other.

Using Aristotle's peculiar definition, it appears that Herodotus cannot be engaged in anything other than 'an imitative art' and hence, even as prose, his work would qualify as poetry. However, it might be argued that he was disqualified because Aristotle did not see his work as wholly 'imitative': the historian may make use of his imagination, but at the core of his work is a factual or interpretative base which is the common currency of his craft. The historian's representation is circumscribed by things which are known or are assumed to be known: he cannot, in his capacity as an historian, deliberately devise 'fictions' which are contrary to received wisdom or accepted truths, and he must submit his work to the scrutiny of his fellows, whose function is to expose omissions, errors of fact, distortions in interpretation, inadequacies in methodology, and fallacies in argument. In these limitations he is more akin to the physicist than to the purely creative artist, for the latter's productions are bounded only by physical constraints and the potentialities of his fancy and/or imagination; and, this being so, it did make some sense for Aristotle to distinguish between the respective 'imitations'. But he went further than this by claiming that poetry was 'more philosophic and of graver import than history', and thereby he created more difficulties.[6] The word 'philosopher' derives from two Greek words which together mean 'a lover of wisdom', and Greek philosophy is often interpreted as a search for knowledge for its own sake, particularly in the contrasting spheres of moral and natural philosophy, which have come down to us as ethics and physics. As Aristotle specifically excluded physics from his 'imitative arts', his claimed importance for poetry lay in the sphere of moral philosophy, or in the principles and nature of individual and community conduct. Yet history in its representations of the once-real past provides countless practical examples of the whole range of individual and community characters, activities and inter-relationships, while the unifying principle of cause and effect affords a pragmatic approach to systems of ethics by demonstrating consequences in both the short and long run, and for both individuals and societies. There can be no logical reason why such representations and demonstrations should be thought to have less moral significance than those which may have little foundation in reality and which may be wholly the products of reason. Accordingly, it could be argued that any deficiencies that Herodotus displayed with respect to the 'imitative' nature of his art were more than compensated for by the philosophic implications of his work, and that on that account he would have an additional claim to be a poet while he was still in prose.

What, however, if he was changed into verse of a tolerably good quality? Aristotle's view that the resulting work would still be history and not poetry makes sense only if the prevailing orthodox definition of poetry is abandoned and his own is substituted. On the orthodox definition, the only change necessarily involved in the transformation would be the substitution of verse metre for prose rhythm, and this change alone would establish the status of the work as poetry. On Aristotle's definition, where poetry became 'an imitative art' or 'the making of fictions', the assumed 'real' or 'factual' content would preclude the status of poetry. As contemporary opinion held that both fact and fiction could be put into verse, then on this Aristotle was the odd man out, and his new definition was clearly untenable. Further, his attempt to establish the status of his 'new poetry' as the purveyor of a superior form of moral philosophy was equally misguided, since ethical systems derived from and testable by 'real' facts and situations must ever be better grounded than those which originate as abstractions and must ever reside only in the realms of theory. Prose and poetry were terms relevant to the organisation of oral and written communication: they did not signify systems of ethics, nor the principles from which these had been derived.

Fortunately, the following centuries continued to write their histories in both prose and verse, and saw the latter as a form of didactic poetry which they could listen to or read for both pleasure and profit. Their 'profit' might include not only factual knowledge but also the moral instruction that may be gained through the study of the practical example.

(C) WORDSWORTH AND THE MEANING OF POETRY

Wordsworth's Preface was thoroughly revised and enlarged for the Third Edition of *Lyrical Ballads* in 1802, and it forms a coherent and closely argued manifesto which explains and defends his views on the processes involved in his poetic compositions and on the language in which these should be written.[7] It has lengthy passages on the relationship between poetry and prose, and is saturated with his views on the importance of poets and poetry to the world in general. It has had great influence, and it repays close study.

Like Aristotle, Wordsworth tried to overthrow the existing conceptions of poetry and prose as opposites. He repeatedly minimised any distinction between them, and saw little if any difference between the metre which he found in prose and that found in verse. In a footnote, he explained that his own use of the word 'poetry' to contrast metrical compositions with prose was 'against his own judgement', and he continued as follows:

'Much confusion has been introduced into criticism by this contradistinction of Poetry and Prose, instead of the more philosophical one of Poetry and Matter of Fact, or Science. The only strict antithesis to Prose is Metre: nor is this, in truth, a strict antithesis, because lines and passages of metre so naturally occur in writing prose that it would be scarcely possible to avoid them, even were it desirable.'[8]

Wordsworth thus freed the word 'poetry' for other meanings. In his third paragraph he stated that he saw his poetry as a branch of philosophy, 'well adapted to interest mankind permanently, and not unimportant in the quality, and in the multiplicity, of its moral relations', and he enlarged on this theme later:

'Aristotle, I have been told, has said that poetry is the most philosophic of all writing – it is so – its object is truth, not individual and local, but general and operative; not standing upon external testimony, but carried alive into the heart by passion; truth which is its own testimony, which gives competence and confidence to the tribunal to which it appeals, and receives them from the same tribunal. Poetry is the image of man and nature.'[9]

He further expanded this with what are often considered his most eloquent passages, stating that the poet writes only in his capacity as a human being, and considers 'man and nature as essentially adapted to each other, and the mind of man as naturally the mirror of the fairest and most interesting properties of nature'. He continued by contrasting 'the knowledge' of the poet with that of the man of science, stating that the poet:

'… rejoices in the presence of truth as our visible friend and hourly companion. Poetry is the breath and finer spirit of all knowledge. The Poet is the rock of defence for human nature; an upholder and preserver, carrying everywhere with him relationship and love. In spite of difference of soil and climate, of language and manners, of laws and customs; in spite of things silently gone out of mind, and things silently destroyed; the Poet binds together by passion and knowledge the vast empire of human society, as it is spread over the whole earth, and over all time. Poetry is the first and last of all knowledge – it is as immortal as the heart of man.'

Wordsworth eventually concluded by returning to his opening theme, reiterating that 'if his purpose were fulfilled, a species of poetry would be produced which is genuine poetry; in its nature well adapted to interest mankind permanently, and likewise important in the multiplicity and quality of its moral relations'.[10]

Reading what Wordsworth himself described as 'that sublime notion of Poetry which I have attempted to convey' might seduce many into supporting his views. This would be unwise, since his argument is based on a fallacy, and the subsequent reasoning is unsound. Wordsworth has done little more than adapt the views of Aristotle. Like him, he denied the validity of the orthodox definitions of prose and poetry which saw them as merely contrasting forms of communication. Again like Aristotle, he produced a definition which separated poetry from metre: the latter became the 'antithesis' to prose, while the 'contradistinction' to poetry became 'matter of fact, or science', thus serving the same function for him that Empedocles and Herodotus had served for Aristotle. Still following the latter, Wordsworth saw his poetry as the result of a peculiar kind of creative process, though he replaced Aristotle's 'imitative art' by his own 'colouring of imagination' thrown over 'emotion recollected in tranquillity'.[11] Lastly, he too claimed a philosophic justification for his poetry: it was 'the image of man and nature', the embodiment of a system of metaphysics which encompassed and was superior to all other forms of knowledge, and which subsumed within itself universal and eternal moral truths. The arguments against this line of reasoning have already been advanced in my analysis of the views of Aristotle; however, there are supplementary comments which must be made with reference to Wordsworth alone.

In the first place, much of the argument advanced by him is in the form of generalisations which take the grammatical form of facts, but which are in reality mere assertions, statements of opinion, or matters of belief. Most are completely unsubstantiated; some are so nebulous and/or ambiguous that it is unclear what kind of evidence could ever be furnished either in their support or otherwise; and others can be shown to be wrong. For example, it is not self-evident that the 'object' of poetry is 'truth'. There is not, and never has been, an obligation on a poet *qua* poet to refrain from falsification or fabrication. In this respect the poet differs from the historian, for the latter does have a professional obligation to be impartial, and the search for the most accurate story of the past is generally accepted as the *raison d'être* of his craft. The historian, therefore, has a better claim than a poet to be described as a communicator of truth.

Secondly, Wordsworth provided no evidence for his contention that 'humble and rustic life' produces men who are more in harmony with 'the primary laws of our nature' and Nature's own 'beautiful and permanent forms'.[12] Laws of Nature are capable of a variety of interpretations, and while Wordsworth seems to have borrowed Rousseau's idea of 'The Noble Savage' and applied it to contemporary England, this was an idealistic conception which differed greatly from the reality of the increased pauperisation and demoralisation of England's rural labourers, particularly after 1795. Further, Thomas Hobbes saw the first Law of Nature as an individual and unceasing lust for power that was only extinguished by death; Adam Smith saw it as the enlightened self-interest which formed the bedrock of a free market economy; Thomas Malthus saw it as the natural tendency of population to breed faster than its means of subsistence could be increased; and Social-Darwinists were later to argue that the only beneficent Law of Nature was that which could be summarised in the slogan, 'The Survival of the Fittest'. It is a truism that both man and nature may sometimes be sadly lacking in love – man may by nature be evil as well as good, while nature herself may be 'red in tooth and claw'.

Thirdly, there is no empirical evidence to support Wordsworth's view that poets are 'endowed with more lively sensibility, more enthusiasm and tenderness, a greater knowledge of human nature, and a more comprehensive soul' than other men, or that poets as a class possess a love for humanity greater than that displayed by any other grouping.[13] Ignoring questions arising from the concept of a soul, it must be said that there is no reason to believe that a poet *qua* poet will feel love, a personal incapacity, or the death of his wife more deeply than any other lover, or handicapped or bereaved person; or that a poet *qua* poet will be in any way morally superior to anyone else. On the first point, the fact that poets like Elizabeth Barrett Browning or John Milton may express their emotions better in verse is mainly a reflection of their skills as poets; it is not an indicator of the depth of their emotions relative to others in a similar position.[14] And on the second point, the class of philanthropists is not synonymous with the class of poets, and many of the latter are anyway thought to have possessed personal qualities which allowed them to exempt individuals or groups from their presumed general love of humanity. Poets as diverse as Henry Skelton, Lord Byron, T. S. Eliot, Ezra Pound and Ted Hughes have had aspects of their characters and opinions brought into question, while if the advice given by Larkin in *This be the Verse* were to be followed by everyone, the human race itself would soon be extinguished.[15]

It is now possible to sum up my conclusions with respect to the views of Aristotle and Wordsworth on the relative merits of history and poetry as branches of knowledge, and on whether history put into verse should be regarded as history but not poetry. Whatever may be said in favour of or against the idea of history as a science, it cannot be denied that academic history is a systematic form of study and that the professional historian is a seeker after truth. Poetry, on the other hand, is merely a form of oral or written communication in metre which offers an alternative to the spoken language or to literary prose: it has no status as a branch of knowledge or as a system of ethics, and a poet is not obliged to refrain from the construction of fictions. It is clear, therefore, that history is the superior form of knowledge, and that history presented in metrical language will be poetry as well as history. Even if the material communicated met the most rigorous standards of historical scholarship, and even if the poet deliberately chose to avoid all stylistic devices except metre, this would still be the case – writing in metre in itself would be the sole determinant of whether the work should also be regarded as poetry.

There is nothing in my *Vindication of Miners* which could not be substantiated by reference to contemporary source materials or modern economic theory: it is a didactic poem which can trace its lineage back to Anglo-Saxon England. My second long poem, *The Dreamscape History,* is the product of fact, conjecture, fiction and falsehood, and while parts can be justified by primary and secondary sources, overall it is clearly a work of imagination. Aristotle would have accepted this as poetry because he would have seen it as a work of 'imitation', but his reasoning would have been faulty. The work is poetry, but this is because it has been written in metre, and has nothing to do with the contents. It should be seen as following in a long English didactic but also satirical tradition.

Although I have taken issue with Wordsworth respecting his conceptions of both poetry and poets, I have to confess that I find it easy to see why he has so many admirers. Few would see much harm in promoting a professional status for one's work, or in promulgating those qualities and values which one sees as basic to all humane societies and which one's current environment seems to be repudiating. This is especially so if one's claims are accompanied by the production of poems which attempt to break new ground and occasionally contain work of the highest quality. Fortunately, too, Wordsworth had the highest regard for a combination of metre and rhyme when handling pathetic situations and sentiments. His poetry could come as a revelation to other gifted individuals like John Stuart Mill, aged twenty, and recovering from a nervous breakdown.[16] He could speak for millions when he lamented 'what man has made of man'; when he affirmed that 'we have all of us one human heart' and he celebrated 'its tenderness, its joys and fears'; and when he protested against 'our meddling intellect, mis-shaping the beauteous forms of things'.[17] Lastly, he should not be blamed for later developments over which he had no control: I am sure that he would have been as appalled as I am to read some of the creative writing which is today dignified with the name 'poetry'.

Having said that, however, there is one respect in which Wordsworth laid himself open to criticism. On 21st May, 1807, he re-stated to Lady Beaumont by letter 'that every great and original writer must ... himself create the taste by which he is to be relished', which seems innocuous enough until it is realised that what he wanted was a critical reappraisal of all existing British poetry, as he had previously argued in *Lyrical Ballads*. According to him, much of this fell below the standards he was setting and was 'incapable of exercising the nobler powers of the mind', whereas his own poetry was, as already quoted, 'genuine poetry, in its nature well adapted to interest mankind permanently, and likewise important in the multiplicity and quality of its moral relations'. Hazlitt, in his *Spirit of the Age*, 1825, drew attention to Wordsworth's 'high and severe … almost exclusive standard' of poetry, claiming that it was 'mortifying to hear him speak of Pope and Dryden whom, because they have been supposed to have all the possible excellences of poetry, he would allow to have none'. Wordsworth was to claim in later life that he had been misrepresented by Hazlitt, but his disparagement would tie in with his views on his contemporary, Crabbe, whose early poems had earned the approval of Dr. Johnson for their realism but whom Wordsworth accused of lacking imagination and of writing 'mere matters of fact'. 'I am happy to find that we coincide in opinion about Crabbe's verses,' he wrote to Samuel Rogers from Grasmere on September 29th, 1808. 'For poetry in no sense can they be called … The sum of all is that 19 out of 20 of Crabbe's Pictures are mere matters of fact; with which the Muses have just about as much to do as they have with a Collection of medical reports, or of Law cases.' Crabbe died in 1832 but before this Wordsworth's jealousy of his popularity among contemporary critics led him to tell stories that illustrated Crabbe's lack of imagination, to assert that he preferred the company of women because he had little to contribute in the company of men, his talk being 'trifling', and even to question Crabbe's motives for writing poetry in the first place. De Quincy believed that the tide of critical approval was turning in Wordsworth's favour from 1830-35, and when Wordsworth became Poet Laureate in 1843 it confirmed the view of many that his 'nature poetry' was the highest if not the only form of the art. As I have already shown in my Author's Preface, this was unfortunate because it helped in the long run to foster an élitist conception of both poetry and poets together with the idea that didactic poetry is 'a poetic changeling, and not of the true stock'.

(D) PROSE RHYTHM, POETIC DICTION AND MY LONG POEMS

Throughout his Preface, Wordsworth had adopted the accepted distinction between prose and poetry, although (as I have already shown) he believed the true 'contradistinction' should be between prose and metre. He tried as far as possible to minimise any differences between them. He claimed 'that not only the language of a large portion of every good poem, even of the most elevated character, must necessarily, except with reference to the metre, in no respect differ from that of good prose, but likewise that some of the most interesting parts of the best poems will be found to be strictly the language of prose when prose is well written'.[18] Subsequently, he extended this argument: 'We will go further. It may be safely affirmed that there neither is, nor can be, any essential difference between the language of prose and metrical composition.'[19] He put the word 'essential' in italics, and argued that the 'affinity' between prose and poetry was undermined by unnecessary 'verse ornaments' additional to metre and rhyme. It is necessary to consider these views on metre and on diction at greater length.

The English that Wordsworth used had changed greatly as it had evolved from the earliest dialects used in Anglo-Saxon England. By the eighteenth century the related exclamations and sentences through which meaning is expressed could be organised into paragraphs and chapters, the originator being known as a prosaist. In poetry, the exclamations and sentences were organised into lines: a succession of related lines made a stanza, verse or blank verse; a completed work formed a poem; and the author was known as a poet. In general, the pleasing effects of good prose and poetry arise from their rhythms, which have little in common with speech rhythms since they have been reshaped by authors in accordance with the distribution of their stressed and unstressed syllables. The rhythm found in good prose is known as 'prose rhythm': it cannot be described as metrical since it relies on irregularity or dissimilarity, and neither the stresses nor the cadences within a sentence are counted. The rhythm found within poetry, however, is metrical, relying as it does on regularity or similarity, and on the counting of the stresses. Hence, it is determined by the type and number of feet or beats thought appropriate to a line, these feet being counted in terms of their stressed and unstressed syllables. In essence, therefore, the 'strict antithesis' is between prose rhythm and verse metre, and the general antithesis is between prose and poetry. If anyone was confused, it was Wordsworth rather than the critics he was taking to task.

However, he was on much firmer ground in his comments on diction. He saw himself as battling on the one side against critics who could not understand that 'prosaisms' were legitimate and necessary in good poetry, and on the other side against practitioners who were characterised by 'gaudiness and inane phraseology' and 'arbitrary and capricious habits of expression'.[20] The latter adopted artificial devices 'to elevate their style and to raise it above prose', using 'a family language which writers in metre seemed to lay claim to by prescription', and which 'from father to son has long been regarded as the common inheritance of poets'.[21] Yet the only peculiar requirement of poetry was that it should be metrical, with rhyme as an acceptable but dispensable adjunct. The personification of abstract ideas and superfluous poetic diction were two stylistic elements which he would try to avoid, and it was simplicity and directness which should be seen as the main virtues of the language of the poet.

Wordsworth was less than generous to fellow poets who from Caedmon onwards had created elements of style which have given pleasure to millions, but he was correct in seeing metre as the sole requirement for verse, and in believing that poetic diction should depend on the purpose(s) and/or the subject matter(s) of a poem.[22] As already stated in the Author's Preface, my first long poem is an examination of the position of coalminers in the early stages of the industrial revolution and the initial part of the second poem raises many of the academic issues involved in the historical search for truth, or 'historical methodology'. Both poems are didactic in emphasis, having serious and scholarly objectives. They are of considerable length, being 520 and 1,000 lines respectively; they give more weight to analysis than they give to either narrative or description; they embody a conceptual framework or philosophy of history which raises fundamental questions with respect to their wider significance; and they incorporate mindsets and vocabularies which are the stock-in-trade of historians, economists, and political and social scientists rather than poets. Thus, today their factual cores would more often than not be presented in prose, so that if they are to be presented as poetry, they should utilise as far as possible those techniques which are associated with good quality productions of the former. This I have attempted to do.

The poems have titles which indicate their general content, the standpoint of the author, and the status of the discourse as primarily fact or primarily fiction. As in scholarly prose, the contents include the equivalent of an introduction and a conclusion, and the material has been broken down into smaller and more manageable units which are arranged in a logical sequence with a rubric being provided which shows how this has been accomplished. Sections within the poems are conceived of as equivalent to the chapters of a book, and verses within a section are conceived of as equivalent to paragraphs within a chapter. Within the verses, as far as possible the sentences resemble formal prose in their syntax, and their style is simple and direct. As a general rule, there is little recourse to devices like enjambment between verses, colloquial interjections, exotic allusions, repetitions and nonsense phrases or sounds, though I regard inversions and personifications as legitimate and they have been used in both poems. A similar care has been taken with the vocabulary, which has been kept as accessible as possible. However, where technical, specialist or semantically problematic words or terms could neither be avoided nor explained within the text, the prose device of footnotes has been used to overcome this problem. I believe that the combined effect of these features has been to establish a framework that enhances the quality of the verse but also makes the whole poem easier to follow while allowing smaller parts to be more readily remembered and placed within their respective contexts.

(E) VERSE METRE, RHYME AND THE LONG POEMS

It remains to consider the metres, the verse forms, and the rhyme schemes of the long poems. Prosody and centuries of tradition teach that the most suitable foot for English poems of a dignified and didactic nature is the iambus, which is disyllabic and moves from short to long, or from unstressed to stressed. This metre or measure can be traced back to Greek writers of satire, and it was subsequently developed in England as the basic building block for all the principal forms of serious poetry. Shorter lines with few syllables and stresses were used in lyrics and ballads, while the most renowned of the longer lines, the iambic pentameter of ten syllables and five stresses, was always used in epic or heroic poetry, in blank verse and in the sonnet. It is this line which at first sight seems most suitable for my long poems, leaving the basic choice of whether to fashion it in the open pattern of blank verse and the epic, or to adopt a closed pattern like the heroic couplet. These alternatives carry the same inherent danger, namely that hundreds of lines of successive iambic pentameters can quickly become monotonous and boring; and further, that if they are combined with subject matters which themselves require close attention, then they can militate most strongly against the reasons why those subject matters have been presented as poetry rather than as prose. The choice of metre, and the decision with respect to open or closed pattern, have profound implications for the eventual success or failure of the poems.

However, by the end of the fourteenth century English writers already possessed a range of techniques which could introduce variety and counter soporific tendencies, and thereafter lines based on the iambus soon showed an astonishing flexibility. It is believed that the earliest Anglo-Saxon poets had used alliteration and a moving caesura as the principal devices by which the verse rhythm could be kept metrical, and the meaning and syntax of the sentences could be simultaneously maintained. Subsequently, the metre itself could be changed by substitution, that is, by replacing one of the iams by a trochee (disyllabic and going from long to short, or from stressed to unstressed) or a spondee (again disyllabic, but two longs or stressed, and hence relatively rare) at the start of a line. Occasionally, an extra syllable could be added, so that the stress now fell on the penultimate one, producing what is called a feminine line ending. Another technique developed was that of enjambment, which meant that the sentence on one line, instead of being end-stopped, was allowed to run over: it might sometimes occupy several lines or even a whole stanza. And lastly, a very far-reaching innovation was the use of rhyme.

The Norman Conquest had brought the temporary ascendancy of French as the language of written poetry, and by the time that vernacular English was again being used assonance, consonance and rhyme were being copied from French models, while the rhyming couplet was being given an enhanced status by Chaucer. Rhyme in itself added a new dimension. On the negative side, it can be an inhibiting factor with respect to vocabulary; it can lead to distortions in the syntax of a sentence; and the heroic couplet can too often sound as if it is bringing a poem to a premature close. More positively, it also offers opportunities for various forms of stanza; it pleases the ear; it assists the memory; and it draws and holds attention to the meaning or substance of a sentence. Even if there are occasions when it does inhibit vocabulary, it should be remembered that languages are constantly evolving, and that the creation of new words and expressions and the addition of new meanings to existing ones continuously open new possibilities for rhyming. Further, it is widely believed that serious and pathetic subjects are more favourably received when presented with rhyme, and experimental psychology has shown that people are more willing to believe something when it is presented as verse. People neither converse nor write their prose in alliterative iambic pentameters, so that both blank and heroic verse may be described as poetry. But neither do they do these things in rhyme, so that heroic verse may be said to be one step further removed from prose than is blank verse, and hence may be described as 'more poetic' than the latter. On all these counts the heroic couplet seems the most appropriate choice for both my long poems.

In the event, this assessment proved over-optimistic, for experience soon showed that the heroic couplet was far more suited to the content of the first poem than it was to that of the second. The only major problem of form with the first poem was the determination of the size of the individual verse: it was only after repeated experimentation that I concluded that it had to be as long as twenty lines if the advantages which I anticipated would arise from the heroic couplet were to be fully realised. However, this did not work well with important parts of the second poem, and experiments with blank verse not only failed to improve things but also surrendered in advance the advantages to be derived from rhyme. Being unwilling to completely abandon the iambic pentameter or the rhyming couplet, I tried varying the line length and alternating the pentameters with iambic tetrameters, or lines of four feet with four stressed syllables. This also initially proved unsatisfactory, but after trying various permutations I eventually settled on the form in which the poem is now presented. Each verse consists of eight lines made up of four rhyming couplets which act as the building blocks for two quatrains. The first quatrain alternates the iambic pentameter with the iambic tetrameter, thus varying the line lengths and the number of stressed syllables: the second quatrain drops the pentameters and substitutes two more tetrameters, thus giving four consecutive octosyllabic lines. A moving caesura, substitution of the iambus, an extra syllable and enjambment could be used as in the previous poem, as could alliteration, assonance, consonance and end rhymes. This new arrangement proved ideal. I had previously concluded that the difficulties originated from the most analytical parts of the poem, and this verse-form allowed variations in the structure and length of the sentences, and a smoothness in transition from one sentence to the next, both within and between verses, that obviated these problems. Overall, both poems now exhibited closed pattern verse forms and logical developments which in my judgement combined the major advantages of both prose and poetry.

(F) CONCLUSIONS

I have shown that both Aristotle and Wordsworth set out to change the meaning of the word 'poetry' as used by their contemporaries, and that neither provided an adequate justification for this. Further, I have shown that poets *qua* poets are in no way superior as human beings, and that poetry *qua* poetry has no claim to be a branch of knowledge, philosophical or any other. Hence, Herodotus put into verse will be both history and poetry, and historical knowledge cannot be seen as in any way inferior to the 'knowledge' possessed by poets. My long poems demonstrate this, since the first is securely based on the historical record, while the second, though incorporating a considerable number of historical facts, is clearly a work of imagination, or fiction. I have been at some pains to show how the verse metres and forms were determined, thus illustrating the correspondence between their contents and their presentation, and providing a practical demonstration of the principle of 'Fitness for Purpose'. The correspondence between form and metre must always be the most important element in the construction of a poem, for neither emotions, however deeply felt, nor convictions, however sincerely held, can of themselves produce good poetry. Readers must make their own judgements on how successful I have been in my application of this principle.

NOTES AND REFERENCES

1. A. R. Myers, *England in the Late Middle Ages*, p. 82 (Pelican, 1956)

2. E. Wilson, *Is Verse a Dying Technique?*, pp. 22-23, first published in 1938 and reprinted in *The Triple Thinkers* (Penguin, 1962, pp. 22-39)

3. J. M. Cameron, *Poetry and Dialectic*, p. 5. (Leeds University Press, 1961). This inaugural lecture was delivered on 13/3/61 within the University. Professor Cameron cited *Aristotle on the Art of Poetry*, pp. 24, 25 and 43, translated by Ingram Bywater with a Preface by Gilbert Murray (Oxford, 1920)

4. E. Wilson, in loc. cit., p. 23

5. For the former in context, see A. R. Burn, *Introduction to 'Herodotus: The Histories'*, (Penguin, 1972), pp. 7-37; for Empedocles, see Charles Singer, *A Short History of Scientific Ideas* (Oxford, Clarendon Press, 1959), especially pp. 29-31

6. Quoted by Professor J. M. Cameron, in loc. cit., pp. 7-8

7. D. N. Smith (ed.) *Wordsworth: Poetry and Prose* (Oxford, The Clarendon Press, 1924). The Preface is reprinted whole on pp. 150-176, with notes on pp. 210-211, and I have cited subsequent quotations as W. Wordsworth, ibid., followed by the page number or numbers

8. W. Wordsworth, ibid, p. 159

9. ibid, p. 150 and pp. 162-3

10. ibid, p. 163, 164, and 165; p. 17

11. ibid, p. 152 and p. 17

12. ibid, pp. 152-3

13. ibid, p. 161

14. Elizabeth Barratt Browning (1806-1861), Sonnet, 'If thou must love me, let it be for naught'. John Milton (1608-1674), Sonnet XV1, 'When I consider how my light is spent' and Sonnet X1X, 'Methought I saw my late espoused saint'

15. The last line of Philip Larkin's awesomely horrible poem reads: 'And don't have any kids yourself.' See Thwaite, Anthony, ed., *Philip Larkin: Collected Poems* (The Marvel! Press, 1988) p. 180

16. John Stuart Mill, *Autobiography* (World's Classics, Oxford, 1924)

17. The quotes are from 'Lines written in early spring' (1798); 'The Old Cumberland Beggar' (1797); 'Intimations of Mortality' (1800-06); and 'The Tables Turned' (1798)

18. W. Wordsworth, ibid, p. 15

19. ibid, p. 15

20. ibid, pp. 151 and 15

21. ibid, pp. 156 and 15

22. Caedmon's Poem and a translation thereof can be found in K. Baker, ed., *The Faber Book of English History in Verse*, p. 9. (Paperback Edition, London, 1989.)

A VINDICATION OF
EARLY MINERS

A VINDICATION OF
EARLY MINERS

PROLOGUE

SECTION A: In which the Principal Features of Private Ownership and Exploitation are Introduced

SECTION B: In which the Development and Inevitability of Class Consciousness are Analysed

SECTION C: In which Natural and Artificial Controls are shown to lead to Inequality in Class Conflict itself

SECTION D: In which the Errors of a purely Quantitative Approach are Considered

EPILOGUE

PROLOGUE (LINES 1-20)

Pope once discoursed on Man, and to his shame
Declared self-love and social were the same –
A factious fiction greeted with applause
By those kept rich through sanguine class-based laws.
"What is, is right," pontificated Pope,
Thus branding all reform a forlorn hope.
But there were later poets who clearly saw
That rights of property might wrong the poor;
Who agonised as crises came and went,
And wide distress produced great discontent;
And who no 'hastening ills' would leave unsaid
When versifying those who 'pined for bread'.
Now my Muse, too, enjoins me to refrain
From flights of fancy that beguile the brain,
And calls upon my reason to reveal
Those truths the followers of Pope conceal –
Truths that in real experiences reside,
Which, when related, cannot be denied.
The lot of miners I will hence explore,
And readers then may their conclusions draw.

    Ref. 11. 1-6
    Sc/Ref. 1. 11
    Ref. 1. 12

SECTION A

IN WHICH THE PRINCIPAL FEATURES OF PRIVATE OWNERSHIP AND EXPLOITATION ARE INTRODUCED

VERSE ONE (LINES 21-40)

It was the early nineteenth century when
Mistreatment gave a just cause to these men
As deeper and more dangerous mines were drained.
Early, the private owners they arraigned:
Surely, excessive profits these had gained,
And miners' living standards had reduced
Through subtle tricks they over time produced.
"Parsimony's our watchword," they had cried.
For safety measures some on luck relied,
While high-rent houses where they must reside
Kept miners to their masters closely tied.
Clawbacks from wages, too, some finely honed.
These present pays by long delays postponed,
And paid in truck or kind, and others scored
Through Tommy shops where normal prices soared,
And where adulteration added fraud.
Such sharp abuses enmity enhanced.
Thus feelings of class-consciousness advanced
By sabotage, by lock-out and by strike
Which, sadly, bore on good and bad alike.

Sc. 1. 23
Note 11. 32-6
Note 11. 38-39

VERSE TWO (LINES 41-60)

Now miners formed a close community
Which over time had its paternity
In cant-full 'can't-care won't-care' laissez-faire,
And the deterring dreaded workhouse where
Small children from their parents' arms were pulled
And marriage vows were cruelly overruled.
Self-help they found their best security
Against a premature senility,
And obscene levels of morbidity,
And bodies earthed-up for eternity.
No group of workers could there ever be
So conscious of their own mortality,
Their fitful sleep betraying nightmare fears
Death would preclude three-score-and-ten in years.
It might be that his face he would present
Through atrocity, or by accident:
Perhaps some luckier than the rest he'd send
A quick and relatively painless end –
But others, blameless, he'd not spare a fate
That would a host of sadists satiate.

> Note 1.43
> Ref. 11. 44-6
> Sc. 1. 57

VERSE THREE (LINES 61-80)

For allies in his works of woe he found
Fire-damp and choke-damp deep within the ground,
And seismic movements for his ends he took
So he'd be everywhere that they might look.
Death, with snaps and whirrings, as cages fall
And quaking men crouch tightly in a ball.
Death, with cracks and thunder, as props give way,
And pinioned men distorted limbs display.
Death, with splash and swirlings, as water looms
And gulping men thresh wildly in their tombs.
Death, with stealth and squirmings, as gas will seep
And gagging men a dreadful tryst must keep.
Death, with smells and screamings, as fire consumes
And what was human flesh new shapes assumes.
Death, by suffocation, as air turns stale
And gasping men a different gas exhale.
Death, by slow starvation, as food runs out
And bags of skin and bones their Gods may doubt.
And, a cruel and crippling consummation,
Surface death, by coal-dust inhalation.

    Note 1. 62
    Sc. I. 68
    Sc. 1. 76
    Note 11. 79-80

VERSE FOUR (LINES 81-100)

Men shuddering start from sleep such shades supply,
And waking, wonder at the reasons why
Good husbands, fathers, sons and brothers die.
Faith is not lost: heaven has reserved a place
For those whose love has graced the human race.
Love God, and love thy neighbour as thyself,
Are hardly precepts which encourage pelf.
Instead, they underpin a commonwealth
In which privation and adversity
Engender feelings of fraternity.
Where could you ever find a greater friend
Than he on whom you for your life depend?
Where else should orphans and poor widows turn,
If not to those who never would them spurn?
Kin, neighbours, comrades, friends and some unknown
Rally to those bereft or all alone,
While chapels, clubs, choirs, unions and brass bands
Provide a multitude of helping hands.
All safety nets would form, to set at naught
Ordained life-chances of the lesser sort.

Sc/Note 1. 81
Sc. 1. 84
Note 1. 87

VERSE FIVE (LINES 101-120)

Some mutilations and some deaths might seem
The work of Fate, or part of God's Grand Scheme.
But many gave a somewhat different view
And it was mainly from these that there grew
A hatred of that evil frame of mind
Which lives would stake within the daily grind
Provided this helped keep deep pockets lined.
For some charged children with the winding gear
Which took their brethren up and down in fear;
And some the use of safety lamps refused,
Claiming they'd not arrived or were misused;
And some permitted roofs too prone to fall
With too thin pillars and too wide a stall;
And some their pits a second shaft denied
Thus trapping gas and air that's foul inside;
And some kept hempen ropes for far too long
Though those of wire were known to be more strong.
Yet others pinched on props, or failed to drain,
And found a hundred little ways to gain,
Subtracting costs while adding human pain.

Sc. 1. 103
Note 11. 112-3

VERSE SIX (LINES 121-140)

And pain and penance formed the daily lot
Of children with whose work black gold was got –
Children whose suffering far from public view
Surfaced and shocked in eighteen forty-two.
By age, dependence, and by Statute caught,
By parish sent, or hapless parents brought,
They quavered through long frightening days of toil
Where coal-dust formed their substitute for soil,
Until, by carry, stumble, and by crawl,
They homewards went, to sleep in hours small.
And then, summoned too soon from sweet repose,
Back to their mine they trudged, still in a doze.
Infants as young as four were used as cats
To keep the hewers' lunches safe from rats;
While lonely trappers, who'd reached six or more,
Crouched in near darkness, wet beside their door.
Near-naked children carried, pulled, and pushed,
As ladders and steep inclines spirits crushed,
And even those no accidents befell
Bore bodies stunted by their earth-bound hell.

    Sc. 1. 123
    Ref. 1. 124
    Sc 1. 127

SECTION B
IN WHICH THE DEVELOPMENT AND INEVITABILITY OF
CLASS CONSCIOUSNESS ARE ANALYSED

VERSE SEVEN (LINES 141-160)

Though mining horrors have been widely famed,
Not every owner should be named and shamed.
Some simply claimed that they were unaware
Of many banes the miners had to bear.
Others, in conscience, did attention draw
To their good works among the labouring poor.
Most saw the plight of workers as innate,
As something they could only palliate,
A thing that breeding did exacerbate.
Smith, Malthus and Ricardo had all taught
The iron laws of economic thought:
A rise in costs a common ruin would bring;
Wage-rises were a self-defeating thing;
Price rises cause the market share to fall;
It's jobs with risks, or it's no jobs at all.
Such views take competition for their base
But by their nature they concede the case
Of those who would disharmony efface.
For when the profit motive forms the heart,
The body politic is torn apart.

Sc. 1. 146
Ref. 1. 151
Note 1. 153

VERSE EIGHT (LINES 161-180)

This fact trade cycle theory has decreed,
And set short-term parameters for greed,
By pre-determining with in-built gloom
A bust to follow every major boom.
Booms bloat the gap between the rich and poor:
In them, the workers agitate for more.
Depressions mean there's now less in the pot:
In them, workers hang on to what they've got.
Stretched sobering slumps the worst conditions see,
As owners fight the threat of bankruptcy,
And workers, driven by redundancy,
Are further pushed into their poverty.
Against such economic forces vast
Stands capital accrued in good times past.
How then should those unfortunates behave
Whose wage was never big enough to save
In their grim trek from cradle to the grave?
Only their fellows really know their plight,
And they'll conclude this never can be right:
They'll fight a system which entails such blight.

Sc. 1. 161
Note 1. 163
Sc. I. 169

VERSE NINE (LINES 181-200)

Its axiomatic struggles will ensue
As booms and slumps in turn themselves renew,
And therefore it should be of no surprise
That they increase in frequency and size
As national trends the local ones subvert
And every region finds it suffers hurt.
'Survival of the fittest' is the name
By which apologists admiring came
To laud the waste and pour scorn on the slain
Involved in this supposed social gain.
Rarely did these great minds really question
Whether lock-out and elimination
Would augment the union of the nation.
In truth, the morals of the market place
Those of a pack of wolves would not disgrace.
Employers red in tooth and claw soon find
It's easy to take over those more kind;
While workers diligent and never late
With those more feckless share a common fate –
And learn such bad faith not to tolerate.

    Sc. 1. 181
    Sc. 1. 185
    Sc. 1. 190

VERSE TEN (LINES 201-220)

Two other vicious trends will also toil
The axles of disharmony to oil.
First-born sons increasingly inherit
Wealth for which they need display no merit –
As seen when monarchs dying pass their crowns
To heirs who turn out imbeciles or clowns.
To unfit owners hardly worth the name
Blind capital then adds a deeper shame,
Unweeping for the havoc which it wreaks
As maximum returns it heedless seeks.
This monied interest industry transcends:
All other factors to its will it bends
As capital from coast to coast it sends,
And native jobs to other countries lends.
Now, owners know that finance loves them not,
And will desert as soon as things get hot;
Yet by her side they still their stand will take
If common foes the system try to break.
For power's then at stake. When power's at stake,
They'll grit their teeth and lifelong friendship fake.

    Sc. 1. 211
    Sc. 1. 219

VERSE ELEVEN (LINES 221-240)

Cohesive currents that emerge and surge
Combine the discrete units to converge.
Dissentient voices everywhere are urged
Their own proclivities must be submerged,
And any counter-tendencies be purged.
Land, capital and those who organise
Quickly their common interests recognise.
Labour, more graded, tends to lag behind:
Unskilled with skilled are difficult to bind,
As are part-time and casual workers, too,
Since fear for them provides a stronger glue.
Each class its own identity presumes:
Its language soon class-consciousness assumes.
Then each an ideology creates:
A mindset of division permeates.
On this cleavage class hatred richly feasts:
Class enemies are demonised as beasts,
Or worse; and every strain and hurt are nursed
And over years their finer points rehearsed
Until as class-based scourges they are cursed.

Sc. 1. 227

VERSE TWELVE (LINES 241-260)

This chasm by Disraeli was deplored
When he his own society explored.
Two separate nations side by side he penned,
And few did any empathy extend.
But his division into rich and poor
Meant that a discreet curtain he could draw
Over the thing that mattered even more.
For the determinant, without a doubt,
The thing the lower orders were without,
The thing without which they were daily done
And knew deliverance could not be won,
The thing that counted every single hour,
Was power – their utter lack of any power.
Power's not a purring word. It's hard and short.
Pundits its connotations have long sought,
And finer points to its relations brought.
'Power and authority'. 'Power and control'.
Majestic books from printing presses roll!
Yet, when the masses are to be contained,
Two powers only need to be maintained.

    Ref. 1. 242
    Sc. 1. 243
    Sc. 1. 253
    Sc. 1. 254
    Sc. 1. 257

SECTION C
IN WHICH NATURAL AND ARTIFICIAL CONTROLS ARE SHOWN TO LEAD TO INEQUALITY IN CLASS CONFLICT ITSELF

VERSE THIRTEEN (LINES 261-280)

Nature herself the first power did contrive,
For men must eat if they're to stay alive.
No artificial government or creed
Can match this tyranny of innate need,
Nor is there anything that men won't do
When preservation is the end in view –
A spur that never will more deeply rake
Than when dependants also are at stake.
Now, if demand for jobs outruns supply,
Employers previous gains will nullify.
Pay, contracts and expensive safety rules
Will be perceived as temporary tools;
Concessions from cowed workers will be sought,
And harshly they a heavy lesson taught.
Necessity's the wet-nurse of this trend.
Unwilling workers will be made to bend
As day by day this truth they comprehend:
'Rather as wage-slaves than as paupers fend!'
Advantage, then, in long industrial strife,
Remains with him who need not risk his life.

Sc. 1. 261

VERSE FOURTEEN (LINES 281-300)

The second power from men themselves derives,
And like the first it dominates men's lives.
Its scope extends to making lethal law,
And, through this, that of ruling rich and poor.
Suppose by law itself this power was tied
To a minority, by wealth allied.
A partial regulation of class war
That proud and raised élite could now ensure,
And proper scales of punishment reverse
By a proportionality perverse
That values life at less than one cut purse.
A breach of contract could be made to be
An unfair act of criminality,
With gaol for workers a reality.
Strikes, demarcation disputes and go-slows
Might legally be dealt some bruising blows.
Strikes could be banned: or, if they were allowed,
Strikers themselves be deemed part of a crowd,
And classified as a conspiracy
Which threatened lives and other lunacy.

Sc. 1. 281

VERSE FIFTEEN (LINES 301-320)

Our old religion which in former days
The economics of the Schoolmen praised,
Could to a newer ethic give the nod,
And trim and turn unto a sterner God
Who earthly profits managed to combine
With prophecies of higher gains divine.
Fallacies that centuries had compounded
By self-interest now could be confounded.
Hours, apprenticeships, machines and wages
Could de-regulated be by stages.
Just prices just a heresy could seem –
The converse of His beneficent scheme
That market mechanisms deemed supreme.
Regrators and forestallers one could bless:
Their acumen in business one could stress.
Enclosers and engrossers one could laud:
Such enterprise deserved a rich reward.
And usurers, whom everyone abhorred,
Had been maligned by inverse logic flawed:
Debtors won't borrow what they can't afford!!

Note 11. 301-6
Sc. 1. 307
Sc. 1. 308
Note 11. 311-320

VERSE SIXTEEN (LINES 321-340)

Informal controls were already fact.
Job allocation in itself would act
To instil that degree of deference
Which guarantees a guilt-free reference.
Formal controls could pose a greater threat.
These would allow the government to net
A group of workers at one go; and let
Them break their bracing solidarity
By setting them against society.
Work uncompleted might not so be left,
Nor other workers from their masters cleft.
On subtle secret oaths these laws could frown.
For pickets, maximums they could lay down,
And should they obstruct or intimidate,
To further laws they'd be subordinate.
Employers' capital could be assured
By a death penalty through law procured,
Though union funds would not be so secured.
Cheap mobile labour, too, they could ensure:
Relief would go to paupers, not the poor.

Note 1. 340

VERSE SEVENTEEN (LINES 341-360)

In fact, the power to make the law was tied
To a minority, by wealth allied;
And that minority did use the law
For partial regulation of class war.
Thus law the rights of property upheld,
And law the rights of working men repelled;
And since on public record laws now lie,
Apologists their sanctions can't deny.
So they now on a different point expound,
And claim these laws that were in statute found,
Being seen as mainly a dead letter,
Proved in fact the laxest form of fetter.
Further, they claim that anyway it's wrong
To think that anti-union laws when strong
Can have effects upon the wage-rates paid,
And hence put market forces in the shade.
Such ineffectiveness, they state, is clear
From years when Acts supposedly spread fear.
For in those years the miners did quite well:
Their general living standards rose, not fell.

    Sc. 1. 341
    Sc. 1. 349

VERSE EIGHTEEN (LINES 361-380)

As living standards must be analysed
By means of methods specially devised,
It's best for now to push them to one side,
And deal with law as it was then applied.
For law is law until it is repealed,
And law thought dead is really law concealed.
Thus, a 'dead letter' law against French spies
Could later be exhumed and utilised
Against farm workers, and could them transport –
Alongside felons of the grossest sort –
To a bleak servitude they had not earned,
And from which only lucky ones returned.
Power made that law, and law example made,
And workers knew to ever be afraid.
Now if, as claimed, law's impact was so small,
Then why have anti-union laws at all?
Further, if miners' living standards rose
Despite those laws designed to this oppose,
Then might not greater rises have been seen
If anti-union laws had never been?

Note 11. 361-4
Ref. 11. 367-72
Sc. 1. 373

SECTION D
IN WHICH THE ERRORS OF A PURELY QUANTITATIVE
APPROACH ARE CONSIDERED

VERSE NINETEEN (LINES 381-400)

It's now incumbent to investigate
Some major features of that grand debate
Which claims that living standards can be traced,
And that conclusions can be on them based.
Despite the methodology that's framed,
This is not half as certain as is claimed.
Some chose – for fervour common sense outran –
To postulate an 'average working man'.
They then progressed unto a second stage:
This average man must have an 'average wage'.
Next, how this wage was spent they must surmise:
Hence, they would need an 'average family size',
And for this fiction budgets would devise
From which essential items they would prise.
These items they'd re-order and would 'weight',
And to them Index Numbers allocate,
While prices over time they'd tabulate,
And thus the Cost of Living calculate.
From this they claimed 'Real Wages' they could draw,
And over living standards they could pore.

Sc. 1. 388	Note 11. 395-6
Sc. 1. 390	Note 11. 399-400
Sc. 1. 392	

VERSE TWENTY (LINES 401-420)

Ingenious are these methods which they use,
The gullible to influence or confuse;
And timeless are the troubles that they take
When series, tables, charts and graphs they make.
Their work in science seeks a strong ally:
On economic concepts they rely,
And strengthen their mad urge to quantify
With dubious algebraic formulae.
They don't equate statistics with 'damned lies':
Objective truths from them alone arise.
Accordingly, when figures they espy,
They close their heart and open their right eye,
And try then to belittle or deny
Those truths that other sources testify.
Presumptuous names these warriors arrogate.
As 'Optimists' or 'Modernists' they prate,
And surely serve to demonstrate how blind
Are zealots when they have an axe to grind.
For, seeking previous work to re-appraise,
Real people from their books they must erase.

    Sc. 1. 401
    Sc. 1. 408
    Sc. 1. 415

VERSE TWENTY-ONE (LINES 421-440)

Instead, they safer sets of figures find
In those dead averages that they've designed,
And, firm in their opinion, pay no heed
To those who say such figures may mislead.
Imagine I met going to St. Ives,
Ten two-legged hale and hearty working wives,
With ten less hearty following behind
Who by one leg to wheelchairs were confined.
There is no 'average wife' within this set,
Since all just one leg and a half would get!
The 'average working man' that some conceive
Is also a result of make-believe,
And lumps together casuals and unskilled
With craftsmen who with pride in work are filled.
And with regard to 'average family size',
Children in decimals they fantasise,
Discounting one thing all mere parents know –
That children prove more costly as they grow.
'Abstractions', therefore, hardly help their cause:
They nourish indices with in-built flaws.

    Sc. 1. 422
    Sc. 1. 429
    Sc. 1. 431
    Sc. 1. 435

VERSE TWENTY-TWO (LINES 441-460)

For as there is no 'average working man',
So there can be no 'average wage' to scan.
Those paid in coin, or money that's received,
As 'nominal' by many are perceived –
Though this should not be thought their work to mar,
Since nominal is what they really are.
Though their reliability be known,
And they in faultless sequence can be shown,
It's nigh impossible to re-create
All circumstances which to them relate.
Was this a skilled or unskilled rate of pay?
Was work done full-time, part-time, or by day?
Was work by quantity, or stint, or chime?
Did it remain a constant over time?
Were perquisites additional to sums paid?
Were fines or other in-house clawbacks made?
Did it both parents and their bairns engage,
Thus making it in fact a family wage?
And, when all sources local scales attest,
Can it in series represent the rest?

    Sc. 11. 441-2
    Sc. 1. 458

150

VERSE TWENTY-THREE (LINES 461-480)

Those prices which as witnesses they call
Are but another sword on which they fall,
Because few series which exist today
Are meaningful in any telling way.
Production prices have to be ignored,
For in the hands of middle-men they soared,
And though on farmers' corn the people fed,
It was the bakers' price they paid for bread.
And, if a series is to be thought sound,
In one place only it has to be found.
For land and water transport then entailed
That it was regional prices which prevailed,
While on these differing levels were imposed
Movements which seasons in themselves composed.
And sometimes short-term factors could hold sway
And cause price changes by the week or day.
Thus, rumours of poor harvests while they're rife,
And threats of foreign wars or civil strife
Led some to hoarding and to panic buys
Which quickly engineered a further rise.

Sc. 1. 472
Sc. 1. 473

VERSE TWENTY-FOUR (LINES 481-500)

The quality of goods must stay unchanged
Over those years that prices are arranged,
While quantities which are to them attached
Must be with equal accuracy matched.
But these provisos have no relevance
When purely local scales take precedence;
When tokens, Tommy-shops, and truck abound,
And much adulteration would be found;
And where the weights and measures utilised,
Had not as yet been wholly standardised.
Further, budgets and averages can't count
Vicissitudes which real life must surmount,
Nor show how qualitative factors changed
As industries themselves were rearranged.
Under and unemployment were a curse;
Births, illnesses and deaths might prove much worse;
Housing and sanitation caused despair;
And smoke and soot polluted once-fresh air.
Thus, annual indices insult the fears
Of those who struggled on by days, not years.

    Sc. 1. 491
    Sc. 1. 499

EPILOGUE (LINES 501-520)

The lot of miners which has been my theme
Was partly due to increased use of steam.
By eighteen-thirty there could be no doubt
That power from harnessed steam had brought about
A revolution in the former way
Men organised themselves for work and play.
But there was little play for Britain's sons
When hearth and engine swallowed coal by tons,
And every year more hewers were required
To risk their lives to keep the boilers fired.
The hardest of all hearts can be dissolved
By details of the tragedies involved –
Though from such evidence this work is free,
Since reason makes this case for sympathy.
My verses show the miners in the mass
As part of an excluded working-class,
As victims whose brave fights for better times
Were often labelled anti-social crimes.
But, with 'deep learning' and a poet's pen,
I've undermined the case against these men.

    Sc. 1. 504
    Ref. 1. 519

REFERENCES (REF.), NOTES AND SCANSION (SC.)

PROLOGUE: LINES 1-20

Ref. 11. 1-6: Pope, Alexander (1688-1744), Poem: *An Essay on Man addressed to St. John, Lord Bolingbroke*, 1733-34. The quotations are adapted from the Epilogue.

Sc./Ref. 1. 11: Hastening: Hast'-ning[2]: Goldsmith, Oliver (1730-1774), Poem: *The Deserted Village*, 1760, l 51

Ref. 1. 12: Crabbe, George (1754-1832), Poem: *The Village*, 1783, l 59

SECTION A: LINES 21-140
VERSE ONE, LINES 21-40

Sc. 1. 23: dangerous: dang'-rous[2]

Note 11. 32-6: 'Long Pays' allowed owners to reduce the need for working capital by paying wages only after the coal had been sold. Paying in coal itself transferred the burden of marketing to the miners. Paying in non-transferable tokens redeemable only in 'Tommy' shops (i.e. those owned or controlled by the mine-owners) eliminated potential consumer choice and thus facilitated higher prices, short measures and adulteration.

Note 11. 38-39: It is now established that the major elements of an adversarial 'industrial relations system', formerly characterised by early scholars as 'collective bargaining by riot', existed half a century before the start of the traditional industrial revolution period.

VERSE TWO, LINES 41-60

Note 1. 43: 'Laissez-faire' is the standard shorthand for 'laissez-faire, laissez-passer', a phrase coined by eighteenth century French economists which translates colloquially as 'leave things alone'. It designates a philosophy which advocated that governments should intervene as little as possible in economic and social life, the latter being left to the operation of market forces through the laws of supply and demand.

Ref.11. 44-6: The clauses referred to took their authority from the New Poor Law (1834). The Church of England marriage service included the injunction: 'Those whom God hath joined together let no man put asunder'.

Sc. 1. 57: luckier: luc-kier[2]

VERSE THREE, LINES 61-80

Note 1. 62: Firedamp, mainly methane (marsh gas) was liable to explode when mixed with air; choke damp was inert and threatened a slow and stealthy suffocation.

Sc. 1. 68: pinioned: pi-nion'd[2]

Sc. 1. 76: different : diff-rent[2]

Note II. 79-80: Now legally recognised as silicosis, an industrial disease for which compensation may be claimed.

VERSE FOUR, LINES 81-100

Sc/Note 1. 81: shuddering: shudd-'ring[2]. 'Shade' here carries one of its older meanings, viz, the appearance of a soul after death.

Sc. 1. 84: Heaven : He'v'n[1]

Note 1. 87: 'Pelf' encompasses wealth, riches and money, but is normally used in a pejorative sense, as in, e.g. Sir Walter Scott's poem titled *Patriotism*.

VERSE FIVE, LINES 101-120

Sc. 1. 103: different : diff -rent[2]

Note 11. 112-3: 'Pillar and stall' was a technique which left coal standing in pillars to support the roof, the stall being the area in which the miner cut, and was found especially in Northumberland and Durham, Cumberland, Lancashire, and Scotland. An alternative system known as longwall mining which used wooden props and removed all the coal was found especially in Shropshire, Staffordshire and Warwickshire.

VERSE SIX, LINES 121-140

Sc. 1. 123: suffering : suff-ring[2]

Ref. l 124: Report, *Royal Commission on the Labour of Women and Children in Mines and Factories,* 1842.

Sc. 1. 127: quavered : qua-ver'd[2]; frightening : fright'-ning[2]

SECTION B: LINES 141-260
VERSE SEVEN, LINES 141-160

Sc. 1. 146: labouring : la-b'ring'[2]

Ref. l 151: The principal elements of the early doctrines of the classical economists were expounded by Adam Smith (1723-90), *The Wealth of Nations*, 1776, Thomas Malthus (1766-1834), *Essay on Population*, 1798, and David Ricardo (1772-1823), *Principles of Political Economy and Taxation,* 1817.

Note 1. 153: The Malthusian Theory of 'The Wages Fund' was based on the fallacy that at any given time the total amount of money available for wages was fixed and that, hence, one group of workers could only be given rises at the expense of the other groups.

VERSE EIGHT, LINES 161-180

Sc. 1. 161: theory : the'-ry[2]

Note 1. 163: The expression 'in-built gloom' is an allusion to the early reputation of economics as 'the dismal science'.

Sc. 1. 169: sobering : so-bring[2]

VERSE NINE, LINES 181-200

Sc. 1. 181: axiomatic : ax-'o-ma-tic[4]

Sc. 1. 185: national : nat'-nal[2]

Sc. 1. 190: supposed : su'-po-sed.[3]

VERSE TEN, LINES 201-220

Sc. 1. 211: interest : in-t'rest[2]
Sc. 1. 219: power's : pow'rs[1]

VERSE ELEVEN, LINES 221-240

Sc. 1. 227: interests : in-t'rests[2]

VERSE TWELVE, LINES 241-260

Ref. 1. 242: Disraeli, Benjamin, Lord Beaconsfield (1804-81), novel, *Sybil, or The Two Nations* (1845)
Sc. 1. 243: separate : sep'-rate[2]
Sc. 1. 253: power : pow'r[1]
Sc. 1. 254: power's : pow'r's[1]
Sc. 1. 257: power : pow'r[1]

SECTION C: LINES 261-380
VERSE THIRTEEN, LINES 261-280

Sc. 1 261: power : pow'r[1]

VERSE FOURTEEN, LINES 281-300

Sc. 1. 281: power : pow'r[1]

VERSE FIFTEEN, LINES 301-320

Note 11. 301-6: 'The Schoolmen' is the collective name given to those pre-Reformation thinkers who codified the rules of economic and social behaviour which have become known as 'applied ethics', the principles which underpinned both canon and statute law. The inter-relationships between Protestantism and Capitalism have been the subject of much academic debate, but it is undeniable that the acceptance of 'economic individualism' meant that by the early nineteenth century the state had abandoned its former rôle, and that 'laissez-faire' was the stock response wherever it was practicable.

Sc. 1. 307: centuries : cen-t'ries[2]

Sc. 1. 308: interest : in-t'rest[2]

Note 11. 311-320: The cornerstone of applied ethics was the idea that wealth was a sacred trust and, hence, the legislation relating to the just price and to usury was designed to prevent one person exploiting those in more need. Legally, until the mid-sixteenth century, only the Jews and then the Florentines could lend money at interest. The just price could be frustrated by forestalling (buying a whole stock of goods before they were brought to market); by regrating (buying and re-selling goods in or near the same market); and by engrossing (buying up large quantities of a good to restrict its supply and thus raise its price above its former competitive level). Thus, for example, in 2013, records were found which show that Shakespeare was repeatedly fined for illegally stockpiling food. Enclosure for sheep farming became a most contentious issue in Tudor England, when it was blamed for rural depopulation and rising corn prices, and Protector Somerset claimed in 1548 that it was encouraged by 'the devil, private profit, self-love, money and such-like the devil's instruments'.

VERSE SIXTEEN, LINES 321-340

Note 1. 340: The Act of 1834 had continued the traditional distinction between the deserving or involuntary poor (i.e. the willing but unable – the aged, the sick and handicapped, and children) and the undeserving or voluntary poor (i.e. the able but unwilling, formerly punished as 'sturdy beggars' or 'idle rogues'). It is often forgotten that at any given moment the majority of the poor were those termed 'the labouring poor', and that these would have been outside the workhouse.

VERSE SEVENTEEN, LINES 341-360

Sc. 1. 341: power : pow'r[1]
Sc. 1. 349: different : diff'-rent[2]

VERSE EIGHTEEN, LINES 361-80

Note 11. 361-4: The relevant quantitative techniques adopted from the discipline of economics, and the difficulties of applying them backwards to periods like the early nineteenth century, are the themes of Section D of this poem.

Ref. 11. 367-72: The reference is to the Unlawful Oaths Act of 1797 which had been passed to curb the activities of French spies during the Napoleonic Wars. The farm labourers of Tolpuddle were uniting against a cut in their wages, and since they had done nothing contrary to the prevailing trade union legislation (principally the Amending Act of 1825 which superceded the Combination Acts of 1799 and 1800), the Unlawful Oaths Act was resurrected in 1834 to ensure that they were convicted and sentenced to seven years' transportation.

Sc. 1. 373: power: pow'r[1]

SECTION D: LINES 381-500
VERSE NINETEEN, LINES 381-400

Sc. 1. 388: average : av-rage[2]

Sc. 1. 390: Ditto.

Sc. 1. 392: Ditto.

Note 11. 395-6: The aim of 'weighting' is to show the relative importance of items found within household budgets. Thus, for example, food, clothing, rent and fuel may be general categories, while bread and shoes may be sub-items within the first two of these.

Note 11. 399-400: It can be seen that whereas tables of 'nominal' or money wages would show only those that were received, tables of 'real' wages would show them in terms of their supposed and re-calculated purchasing power.

VERSE TWENTY, LINES 401-420

Sc. l. 401: ingenious : in-ge-ni'us[3]

Sc. 1. 408: dubious : du-bi'us[2]

Sc. 1. 415: presumptuous : pre-sum'-t'ous[3] ; warriors : war-riors[2]

VERSE TWENTY-ONE, LINES 421-440

Sc. 1. 422: averages : av'-re-ges[3]
Sc. 1. 429: average : av'-rag[2]
Sc. 1. 431: Ditto.
Sc. 1. 435: Ditto.

VERSE TWENTY-TWO, LINES 441-460

Sc. 11. 441-2: average : av'-rage[2]
Sc. 1. 458: family : fam'-ly[2]

VERSE TWENTY-THREE, LINES 461-480

Sc. 1. 472: regional : reg'-nal[2]
Sc. 1. 473: differing : diff'-ring[2]

VERSE TWENTY-FOUR, LINES 481-500

Sc. 1. 491: averages : av'-ra-ges[3]
Sc. 1. 499: annual : an'-ual[2]

EPILOGUE, LINES 501-520

Sc. 1. 504: power : pow'r[1]
Ref. 1. 519: In his poem, *Essay on Criticism*, 1711, 11. 215-6, Pope advises that one should 'drink deeply' of knowledge, since 'a little learning is a dangerous thing'.

THE ONLY DREAMSCAPE
HISTORY OF THE EARLY
ENGLISH STATE IN VERSE

PART ONE

THE ORIGINS AND DISCOVERY
OF
DREAMSCAPE HISTORY

THE ORIGINS AND DISCOVERY
OF DREAMSCAPE HISTORY

SECTION 1

ACADEMIC HISTORY EMERGES AND JUSTIFIES ITSELF AS A
SEARCH FOR HISTORICAL TRUTH

I've shelf on shelf of books that I have read,
Which tell the stories of the dead,
And incidentally earn their authors fame
As players in an endless game
In which each age must always try
Prevailing truths to modify –
Researching ever for a view
To justify the prefix 'new'.

I've further shelves of books which weary me
Through their self-serving honesty,
Which seems their own import to nullify
As they disclaim and qualify.
These always trying tomes unmask
The techniques needed for the task
On which historians are bent,
And all their expertise is spent.

I've yet more shelves of books that I now dread
Which by the previous ones were led
To synthesise the whole of humankind.
Philosophy these call to mind.
Ideas and concepts there are mused,

And with neologisms fused,
And history as she used to be
Becomes a greater mystery.

The authors of these works take great delight
In showing that they're erudite,
While they their other talent keep concealed,
Though in that they may lead the field.
For they've carved a new vocation
In the sphere of job creation,
And through their calling they have found
Employment prospects which astound.

Accordingly, it's apposite to pause
And cogitate upon the cause
Of this vast academic enterprise
That's empire building in disguise.
Scholastics now must be deposed;
Their errors now must be exposed;
Their methods, too, must be made void,
And history once again enjoyed.

* * * * * * * * *

Not for these men those things Antiquity
Prescribed for common memory.
A different grist within their mill they grind,
And in their volumes are inclined
To themes more mindful of their needs
Than tales of great men and their deeds,

Or foreign or domestic strife,
Or chief events in national life.

Clio, once seen as Muse of History
And source of epic poetry,
They judged to literature to be too wed.
'She's cavalier with truth,' they said,
'History for writing's sake is waste;
Her myths offend the modern taste.
While in her hands she holds our fate
We'll never carry any weight.'

Significance they deemed naught but a ruse –
A humbug which their former Muse
Had used to side-line or obliterate
Things they themselves would reinstate.
National identity they'd peel.
Their exposition would reveal
Disunion that on class was based
But race, and gender, too, embraced.

Released from Clio's former claustral chains
They'd seek to fructify their gains
By way of definitions of their own
Which would reclaim this past unknown.
Wide in the margins they would trawl,
And buried truths from there would haul;
And every person, place and thing
Back to the mainstream they would bring.

Easy it is, to discard without tears
Fancies made quaint by passing years:
Harder by far, such conceits to supplant
Without recourse to one's own cant.
In making Truth their only God,
Up a blind alley they now trod:
Soon on this deity they'd gaze
Dazed by a thick semantic haze.

* * * * * * * * *

Though politics, diplomacy and war
They still allowed to be the core,
These areas they thought they would augment
And background features would present.
So they included in their schemes
Social and economic themes,
And divided up the latter
Into discrete subject matter.

Their search for Truth thus spawned a trinity,
And entailed an infinity
Of other disciplines which then evolved
With further problems to be solved.
And as each specialism grew,
Frontiers of knowledge they redrew,
Until there broke a brand-new dawn
With study of the past reborn.

This new Renaissance they'd so carefully sired
New forms of scholarship required,
So those whom diplomatics had sustained,
As polymaths were now retrained.
Theories and methods from outside
To their pet subjects they applied,
And all their quantities revised
Through maths equations they devised.

Yet many of a more parochial sweep
O'er national frontiers would not leap,
And chose, instead, to pluck banalities
From regions and localities.
Hence every city, every town,
Must have their story written down;
And every industry and trade
As 'heritage' must be displayed.

Merry are those whose minds are made to sing
By microscopic modelling,
And happy those who harbour hearts so small
That Hadrian's is their most-known wall.
Pity these men. For at its best
Their life's an unremitting quest
In which each tree they bring to bud
Serves merely to obscure the wood.

* * * * * * * * *

SECTION 2

ACADEMICS DISAGREE ON BOTH THE NATURE AND SIGNIFICANCE OF THIS HISTORICAL TRUTH

Their ideal, Truth, historians have surmised,
From sources only can be prised.
It's from evidence in numerous guises
That well-founded work arises.
From sources '*Who?*' and '*What?*' and '*Where?*'
Are recognised, and then laid bare;
And if the '*When?*' and '*How?*' are meet,
The factual basis is complete.

Now sources start in some unwritten time,
When beings strange stalked in our clime
And left their tracks and relics to decay
And form the records of their stay.
Thus in the strata are dispersed,
And over years may be submersed,
Those plant and animal remains
Which each succeeding age contains.

As time elapsed, and Man came into view,
All types of sources grew and grew.
For tools of stone and bone Man did create,
And by them fought to dominate.
He gathered food from Nature's store;

He hunted game far from a shore;
He painted caves with colours bright
And fashioned objects for delight.

And soon with axes he huge woodlands cleared,
And as part-farmer then appeared;
And he raised earthworks on gigantic scales,
And levelled hills, and reshaped vales.
But extant sources in the field
Few secrets may be made to yield:
It's rare when we can use such finds
To reconstruct our forbears' minds.

Ideas, through which history is laced,
In other sources must be traced.
Oral traditions, fitfully preserved,
And first-hand writings fate conserved,
Allow us now to comprehend
The ways our forbears tried to feud.
Yet even sources such as these
Show Truth as merely one big tease.

* * * * * * * * *

This notion's not to everybody's taste,
And some will now demur in haste.
'The case is over-stated,' they will say,
'For our way is the only way
That history herself can show
Those truths which we would wish to know.

In sources only can be found
An objectivity that's sound.'

'For "history as it happened" is our toast.
Our recreations make the most
Of ways and means which scientists hold dear
And utilise to keep them clear
Of prejudice and bias blind
Which can pollute the human mind.
With rigour we our sources test,
And on the facts our case we rest.'

'The nativity of every item
We research ad infinitum.
Originals we will authenticate.
All copies we investigate,
And fakes we then eliminate,
And folios we then collate.
Thus, we are certain of their date,
And can their provenance relate.'

'When at our explanations we've arrived,
From data only they're derived.
For we see the strength of our conclusions
In avoiding those delusions
Which formulate them in advance
And choose the facts to fit the stance.
And moral judgements we eschew –
On right and wrong we have no view.'

So say the *Relativists*, yet soon they
Are in retreat and some dismay.
For shrewd *Positivists* the floor now take,
And seek a mockery to make
Of those on science who rely
But in their works then this belie
By abnegating as a cause
The idea of inducted laws.

*   *   *   *   *   *   *   *   *

They'll state: 'Your history for history's sake
Is but a spurious claim to make.
Intrinsic grounds alone can never be
Sufficient cause and warranty
For all the effort you expend
On work that seems to have no end,
That fact on fact on fact piles high,
But does not know the reasons why.'

'"The facts speak for themselves," you will contend,
And by this adage you're condemned.
We believe it's self-evidently true
Facts only speak when spoken to.
'Why?' and *'With what result?'* explain
Significance they might contain,
And also show what we should know
For present times which from them flow.'

'From minute details that fatigue the eyes
Broad patterns will one day arise,
Which when subjected to analysis,
Result in an hypothesis.
Now, if this taken is as true,
And then enough of them accrue,
Soon general trends will be produced
And thence a synthesis induced.'

'Thus scientific methods are our key
To understanding history.
Provisional statements are our stock-in-trade,
And lead to models which are made
With preconditions we propose
From which new steps or stages rose.
It's through such theories that we chart
Societies of which we're part.'

Positivists in general laws perceive
A cause in which they can believe.
It's somewhat sad, therefore, that they ignore
The fact that all that's gone before
Has gone before uniquely. For
It can't be logical to draw
From singularities discrete
Laws which prediction will unseat.

*   *   *   *   *   *   *   *   *

SECTION 3

SUBJECTIVE ELEMENTS ARE ANYWAY INHERENT IN BOTH PRIMARY AND SECONDARY SOURCES

Logic, however, both sides should apply
To those 'pure' facts they raise on high.
However neutral facts pretend to be,
They're steeped in subjectivity.
The past was a totality
That had its own reality;
One can't remake it though one would,
Since once it's gone, it's gone for good.

The sources which are held in such esteem
When viewed from other angles seem
Mere accidents. It's sure they are at most
But remnants of a former host
Of evidence sometimes made void,
And sometimes totally destroyed,
By time, perhaps, or mischance wide,
Or those with something dark to hide.

Not only that, but it is also clear
These sources aren't what they appear.
The vast majority of man's affairs
Are of no consequence: so there's
Need only for the things the state

Decides it's useful to create.
'They came, they worked, they went', you see,
Is of most lives a summary.

Seldom can common people write their plight,
Or seek their betters to indict.
Seldom, too, are they honestly portrayed
By those who wish to be obeyed.
So tainted sources from above
Will promulgate with little love
The ideology of those
Who see the masses as their foes.

Now this should not be thought to be unfair
To those who genuinely care.
Their interest in itself can never mean
Their evidence is to be seen
As something of a different hue
That should be treated as if true.
Unconscious bias in it stored
Ensures it, too, is viewed as flawed.

*　*　*　*　*　*　*　*　*

Additional to these problems sources bring,
Others from actual writing spring.
Each individual author will compile
Work in their own peculiar style,
But in so doing will evince
Traits that will make all purists wince,

As they detect on every page
The cultural baggage of their age.

All epochs make a mindset of their own –
One it's impossible to clone,
And one that writers surely can't escape
When pondering how their work they'll shape.
Monastic chroniclers of old
Believed God's purpose would unfold
With miracles from His own hand
Which only He could understand.

More modern ages could not displace God,
Though miracles were seen as odd
By reason, which, to Providence applied,
Would show those laws that therein hide.
Invisible God's hand might be:
Progress, however, all could see.
How then from chaos so malign
Came there an outcome so benign?

Divine and Natural Laws they coalesced,
And found God's Plan was best expressed
In 'laissez-faire', or 'leaving things alone',
Which they were certain could be shown
As vital for free enterprise,
And that self-interest this implies,
And was, besides, the guarantee
Of freedom and democracy.

However, present times sour sceptics bred
Who were to science only wed,
And wrote while tyrannies from left and right
Forced many scholars into flight.
And so professionals still free
Found solace in autonomy,
And mindsets that would underpin
An independent discipline.

*   *   *   *   *   *   *   *   *

Other subjective elements can dwell
Within the works these writers sell.
Some of their native countries are so proud
They sing their praises far too loud
And patriotism they disgrace
Through their presumption that their race
Has been the source of everything
To which a cultured man should cling.

In creeds, another source of bias lies.
The tolerance that's preached soon dies
When wrongs committed, or those that were said,
Are then by ink and paper spread.
So Jews by Catholics were attacked,
While Protestants by both were blacked,
And all on other faiths soon turned
And doubly then with fires burned.

Others, who do not see themselves as fools,
Become beguiled by various schools,
And labels of a most impressive type
They then adopt, their work to hype.
Professionals who to Schools belong
Do not by that alone do wrong:
It's when their politics they shout
That their integrity's in doubt.

Determinists are prone to be dismissed
As steeped in class-based prejudice,
Yet surely should be seen as much preferred
To those who snare through written word.
These claim that in their works there'll be
Only a strict neutrality,
But their productions clearly show
They're wedded to the *status quo*.

Objective Truth can never be regained
When reconstructions are constrained
By most subjective factors of this kind
With which the road to Her is mined.
Bias insidious or overt
Will always honesty pervert,
And even when lies are believed,
That's no excuse to those deceived.

* * * * * * * * *

SECTION 4

ADDITIONAL ACADEMIC ERRORS AND ACTIVITIES LEAD
THE AUTHOR TO DISCOVER AN ALTERNATIVE
DREAMSCAPE HISTORY

Some professionals – determined to abjure
Statements too general or obscure,
And vague impressions wanting to excise
Through methodologies more wise –
Decided they should quantify,
And on statistics should rely,
And books with numbers they should fill,
And then new Truths from old distil.

Cliometrics was the name adopted
For the techniques they co-opted,
And soon econometrics did denote
Those areas in which they wrote.
And as their net they cast more wide
All social sciences they eyed,
And hybrids like psephology
Made part of their pseudology.

'Il faut compter' they took for their command,
Yet rarely seemed to understand
That figures at face value may mislead.
For further heresies they'll feed

Unless it's undeniable
They're valid and reliable,
And, incomplete, won't fail the test
Of representing all the rest.

Defective sources, and those full of gaps,
May force reliance on 'perhaps',
And so imagination must be mixed
With She that on a plinth they've fixed.
Such false conjectures they'll defend
As necessary for their end,
Though really they've just made them up,
As goldsmiths fashion on a cup.

Now, hypotheticals can soon entrance
Those who decode the laws of chance,
And some 'conditional concepts' soon employed
And with them mundane facts destroyed.
They interlaced the 'actual',
With pages 'counterfactual',
And, spell-bound, thought that this should mean
A history as she could have been.

* * * * * * * * *

While fallacies and fancies may displease,
And faults and foibles stir unease,
They underline and illustrate the view
Historians are human, too.
And their Truth's a grand deception,

A most whimsical conception,
A chimera of far-fetched parts
Which in the end will break their hearts.

But presently, there's no such end in sight,
And prospects for the past look bright.
It's not surprising that those who best know
How previous Empires came to grow,
Should use the secrets of their Guild,
And Empires of their own should build
Until so many they deploy
That previous records they destroy.

What bliss to labour in this industry,
With sources that are mainly free!
What joy to realise how these abound
Above as well as below ground!
What comfort is it just to know
That one's materials ever grow,
And do so at so fast a pace
They'll always your own work outrace.

And once a range of sources has been done
There's yet more happiness to come.
Discoveries of importance might be made
Which to old certainties put paid;
Or new techniques are introduced,
And with them salient facts adduced;
And as each age must re-explain,
All sources must be done again.

They get their greatest pleasure from their scheme
When new departments come on stream,
For as old top positions are released
Promotion prospects are increased.
Research becomes their major rôle;
Status becomes their major goal.
And they write books to prove they're smart:
They're both a science and an art.

   * * * * * * * * *

It might be thought that it's not wise to mock
An Empire built on solid rock,
And doubtless this one over which they drool
Is no exception to that rule.
'Everyone has a history'
Is something that all can agree:
This truism, not Truth, sustains
Their crafty and complicit gains.

Herein a paradox which worries lies,
For Empires fall as well as rise,
And surfeits that might seem a wholesome thing
A premature demise might bring.
Their truism that gives such glee
Seduces through simplicity,
And makes no sense unless recast
As 'Everybody has a past'.

For only peoples have a history,
And when researching he and she
It's in biography that we travail.
But this will be to no avail,
Save where upon a wider scale
Our subject and their single tale
Illuminate those things we seek
Which of our national story speak.

Otherwise, there's no discrimination
Or attendant correlation,
And modern scholars seem to be quite mad
As means to ends as ends are clad.
And thus the histories I read
Naught but confusion in me bred,
Until I finished so distraught
That psychiatric help I sought.

And so through therapy I found at last
A new true source that hides the past,
And, with the methodology devised,
Exposes what must be revised.
Memories which in genes now dwell
Our national story wait to tell,
And Dreamscapes only sleep can free
Will give us back our history.

* * * * * * * * *

PART TWO

DREAMSCAPE HISTORY, THE GOLDEN CLASSES AND THE EARLY ENGLISH STATE

DREAMSCAPE HISTORY, THE GOLDEN CLASSES AND THE EARLY ENGLISH STATE

SECTION 1

THE GOLDEN CLASSES CONCEIVE THE IDEAS OF THE NATION STATE AND THE SOCIAL CONTRACT

I stay awake, and in a book I browse
As darkness falls. And then I drowse.
And while I drowse, my mind the past regains,
And sifts and sorts, and then explains.
And histories in genes secured
To fancy's side are now allured,
And memories which dormant lay
At night excite, and have their day.

Dreamscapes provide a history that is seen.
There is no longer 'might have been',
And over sources there's no need to fret –
There's none that's not discovered yet.
Handling skills can be neglected;
New techniques stay unperfected;
Peer reviews need never be sought;
Learned journals never be bought.

There's no pre-booking for a vital source,
Or of a place upon a course;
Nor are there lunch or travel claims to fill,
Nor hotels where there's time to kill.
No foreign or archaic word

Need ever there be read or heard;
No deadlines tight, which can't be met,
There pose to written work a threat.

Since history shown by Dreamscapes is complete,
Authors in style alone compete;
And since performance only needs a bed,
Appraisal is as good as dead.
Yet subjectivity's contained,
And objectivity's maintained,
For Truth her circuit only flies
Within that body where she lies.

My dream engenders one who stands apart –
Though near – divided by his heart,
In which the Goddess Reason fastly dwells
And casts her never-changing spells
At enemies like greed and hate
With which some would her subjugate.
And there's a cloak upon a chair,
And parchments piled up here and there.

* * * * * * * * *

First I see people from another time –
Forbears who slipped primordial slime,
And, waiting for a more auspicious start,
Relied upon the sorcerer's art,
And put their trust in alchemy
From common things to keep them free.

'Til, fired within a different mould,
They saw that only they were gold.

And Golden Ones did they decide to stay,
While keeping baser men at bay;
And golden things did they decide to hold,
While keeping millions in the cold.
And for these ends they deemed it wise
To form a *State*, and then devise
A myriad ways of chaining tight
The countless things they claimed by right.

But soon in Nature raw they found a flaw
Which might restrain their hungry maw.
For though her bounties she could give quite free,
There is of this no guarantee.
So what was needed was a scheme –
An opposite to what it'd seem –
By which the Masses would be left
As victims of *continuous* theft.

And so their brains they racked, and rocked, and rolled,
And found an answer sly and bold:
They'd form a *Nation State*. And then they'd claim,
That all self-interests were the same –
And there ought to be a compact
To be called a Social Contract,
Which, voluntary though it'd be,
Would bind in perpetuity.

This Contract would of Reason seem the fruit
And neatly would their purpose suit.
For their own good the Common Good became,
Which 'neath their banners they would feign.
And Reason saw that in that guise
Social controls she could devise,
Which with discrete social classes
Would subdue the fractious Masses.

* * * * * * * * *

These Golden Ones felt deep within their hearts
That fire which only greed imparts,
And soon I watch them construct in advance
Charts which would clarify their stance.
For they'd seen from the earliest date
That they must differentiate:
And, as division was the key,
They must construct a hierarchy.

Much mathematics on these charts they'd wrought.
They with arithmetic had sought
To nominate, to number, and to slice
From geometric shapes precise –
Like squares, and triangles, and cones,
Which they'd adorned in glaring tones –
Hoping that by calculations
They'd disguise their machinations.

Bisecting was at first their favourite toy,
And was the easiest to employ.
Nature herself it seemed to imitate
By verticals drawn true and straight,
Which, sorting into less and more,
Delineated rich and poor.
But these lines would not clearly show
The ones born high and those born low.

At last, a substitute they deemed as sound
In horizontal lines they found,
And as these in a pyramid they placed,
They skipped and hopped, and their hearts raced.
A top and bottom now were seen
With space for layers in between,
And – here their hearts did nearly stop –
The base was broader than the top.

Thus, they would encompass all the nation
In this one configuration,
Which brought the merit of simplicity
Combined with crude rigidity.
All ranks or classes soon they'd see
Subsumed in national unity,
Subordinate to general rules
Which pre-supposed the Masses fools.

* * * * * * * * *

SECTION 2

THE GOLDEN CLASSES PERSUADE THE MASSES
TO ACCEPT THESE IDEAS

I next see meetings held o'er many years,
When Golden Ones restrained their leers,
And, smirking, said it was to them quite clear
That none should have to live in fear;
That they could curtail deviancy
Through one supreme authority;
And engineers they'd have to be,
And forge a new society.

If the objective was to pacify
Then they would need to stratify;
And if all living standards were to rise,
Then all would have to specialise.
So it would seem, that when needs must,
They should take all the land on trust:
The Mass could work it back on lease,
While they waged war, and kept the peace.

They thus with guile their purposes revealed,
While leaving covert ends concealed.
And then they silent fell. For they knew well,
What cunning said they must not tell:
That War's an underrated care –

A wholesome wheat as well as tare –
Whose stratagems for strangers' lands
Can be applied on native sands.

And pleasing things in Law did cunning find
To aid the aims they had in mind.
Rules of universal application
Would subdue the entire nation.
But linking them to property
Would counteract equality,
And exempt the Golden Classes
From those fates fit for the Masses.

Soon smiles, not smirks, across their faces spread
As by their sophistry they led
The common people to accept a fate
Which when viewed from a later date
Seemed not so much a freedom gained
As numerous other freedoms reined.
Security the Masses sought –
But servitude this Contract brought.

*   *   *   *   *   *   *   *   *

Headmen have things to do: they cannot stay,
And grow impatient at delay.
But Golden Ones have always time to spare:
They've time to play, and time to stare.
And they've got time to frame and hide
Those snares that in small print reside;

And time to execute their scheme
For keeping those like them supreme.

The Headmen, in departing, dissipate:
The Golden Ones remain and prate.
The Man Apart a silent gesture makes –
And one stands up, and water takes.
He clears his throat, and makes a call
For 'Silence Now' from one and all.
He lauds the Contract they've just won,
But warns they've only just begun.

'Experience shows that time's a tiresome thing
Which might unwelcome fortunes bring.
Thus, it must be our Mission to create –
Against the vagaries of fate,
And malcontents enthused by hate –
A panoply from Church and State,
With regulations to ensure
That we stay rich for evermore.'

'Now, we'll need centuries at least before
We can entrap, by war and law,
This obstructive independent nation
Into an inferior station.
But we have skills of management
With which to further our ascent:
Invincible we've always been,
When we've been working as a team.'
'Both in-house and out-source we'll utilise,

And headhunt where best practice lies.
Consultants we'll engage whose expertise
Will be matched only by their fees.
Information we will muster
Using networking through cluster,
And hands-on training we'll cascade
As we fast-track and then regrade.'

* * * * * * * * *

While allusions he had made to staffing
Caused a nervous kind of laughing,
His exposition countering their fears
Called forth from them collective cheers.
With working parties they'd advance
And neutralise the rôle of chance;
And with fine-tuning of their scheme,
They'd hide what they thought it should mean.

Though such euphoria and euphony
Might herald unheard harmony,
Yet motives of the lowest kind can rise
And in the voice shed their disguise.
So now did talk from whispers creep;
And shouts from conversations leap;
And hubbub then with tumult join,
And all a greater discord coin.

Thus a cacophony of trenchant tone
Was first unto the world made known,
And there was nothing in the space around
Which could withstand that awful sound.
Beasts skulked in lairs, and would not rest;
Birds fled the skies, or hid in nests;
Glass shattered into pieces small;
And trees were felled, that once grew tall.

But Golden Ones cared not what Nature thought:
They only cared for what she brought.
Immediately, they former seats resumed,
And then their former charts exhumed.
They formed Committees, and required
That they debate the scheme desired,
And that they furnish with all speed
The resolutions they would need.

From these Committees, Sub-Committees grew,
And these on Working Parties drew.
And Quality Control was then ensured
Through Group, through Sub-Group, and through
Board.
With blueprint drawn, and loopholes closed,
And every composite composed,
They next in plenary sessions meet
And plot both Church and State to cheat.

*   *   *   *   *   *   *   *   *

SECTION 3

THE GREED OF THE GOLDEN CLASSES BEGINS TO SOW
THE SEEDS OF THEIR OWN DESTRUCTION

To head their Nation State they did decree
A masquerade called Monarchy,
And gave it proper nouns like 'King' and 'Queen'
To show its rank, and raise esteem.
It was resolved the King should be
Their one supreme authority,
And that he'd hold for evermore
All powers concerning War and Law.

This King would be surrounded by a court,
And have a Household for support.
He'd have a Council which would him advise:
This would be formed from those thought wise.
All current laws he could extend
If this would Church and State defend,
And offices that power conferred
For Golden Ones would be reserved.

As I observe the Golden Ones debate,
They start to blur, and then vacate.
The Man Apart a new position takes:
He sighs, and signs with both hands makes.
And slowly, slowly, there arise

And pass before my awe-struck eyes
Pageants composed by Kings long dead,
Which by a Crown are proudly led.

Now as these moving pictures substance gain
Their finer details are made plain,
And power and wealth beyond most people's dreams
Provide near universal themes.
Yet my eyes focus on a scene
More mean than scenes have ever been -
A scene that should be passed in haste,
Or banished on the grounds of taste.

This nightmare shows the agonies of Kings.
A sad parade of pain it brings,
As they by sharp vicissitudes are stressed,
And are by stately duties pressed.
On battlement and battlefield,
Their flesh by force they're made to yield;
And torture, murder, and the block
Their once-proud bodies break and mock.

* * * * * * * * *

One spoke for all who suffered by these things.
'We early Anglo-Saxon Kings
Enslaved Romano-Britons still alive.
However, slavery could not thrive
When only captives from outside,
Or our own people courts had tried,

Or strangers we were forced to buy
Formed our main sources of supply.'

'Also, we Kings in fellow Kings espied
Rivals who would not be denied.
Even before the Britons had been crushed
Into each other's lands we pushed.
Then, when our energies we'd spent,
We bowed before the King of Kent,
And, claiming to endorse his fame,
Allowed "Bretwalda" as his name.'

'In fact, as Ethelbert was well aware,
For brute force only we did care;
And "Britain-Ruler" ill-described a man
Whose writ the Thames could hardly span.
Even before this Monarch died
His suzerainty we had defied;
And Raedwald from East Anglia came
And to his title then laid claim.'

'Raedwald proved just another who would vie
In bleeding his compatriots dry,
And by the time the seventh century dawned
A dozen kingdoms had been spawned.
But larger kingdoms swallowed small,
And on each other then did fall:
And soon from Wessex Egbert warred,
And made all England call him Lord.'

''Though no English kingdoms now resisted,
Other Royals still existed,
And these had rival branches of their own
With future troubles thereby sown.
And so the Golden Ones would chafe.
Although their structure might seem safe
Too many Royals would frustrate
Inception of their Nation State.'

* * * * * * * * *

'It seems their blueprint had not understood
The frailties of flesh and blood,
For when investing traits to be admired,
Greed leaves a lot to be desired.
For what can greed but greed sustain?
And why should status her restrain?
And so some Golden Ones declared
That golden things need not be shared.'

'These saw no reason why they should defer
To those who fawning did prefer,
Or those with fancy titles earned through birth
Whose length obscured intrinsic worth.
Hence rose envy, and disrupted.
Internecine strife erupted:
And Golden Ones soon lived in fear
That as a class they'd disappear.'

'Faced with this possibility so fraught,
They sought to give we Kings support
Through genealogy, which could be used
When the succession seemed confused.
Pedigrees they thus constructed;
Lesser lights they then deducted;
And forbears one was proud to see,
Were added to one's family tree.'

'Forgotten facts they brought to light by this.
They rediscovered, with some bliss,
Druids, who once in secret places dwelled,
And who in darker arts excelled.
Teachers and judges these had been,
With brains astute and knives as keen.
But they as priests had mainly plied,
And Celtic peoples terrified.'

'Accordingly, the Golden Ones divined
That heavenly threats must be defined,
And ease the passage of immortal souls
Through earthly sanctions and controls.
Hence, consecration would anoint
Those coronation did appoint:
And sacred relics would secure
Those who were tempted to abjure.'

* * * * * * * * *

SECTION 4

Thus spoke this King, and then, as if on cue,
Prelates appeared whom Mammon knew.
As counsellors and warriors these display,
And strive with fervour to obey
Those who on God's behalf now reign,
And wealth and power bring in their train.
For rights with duties which were owed
Had Reason on all ranks bestowed.

One bishop stands and seeks to justify
The fact that he's been raised so high.
'Consecration seemed a card worth playing
Since it sanctified obeying.
Kingship stays the Church decaying:
Prayers stay the Masses straying.
It's happier times in heaven spent
That keep our earthly poor content.'

'Dear brother, know that when you look on me,
It's darkly, through a glass, you see.
And know that when you search within my heart
You miss the whole, and see the part.
For in my life I can't be seen

God's power and glory to demean:
And though it be a cross I bear,
My status must with God's compare.'

'How should we dress to influence Kings whose laws
See mercy as an alien cause?
And how deport ourselves when meeting those
Who would our office interpose
Between their sins and their one Lord
Who would decree their just reward?
Would not respect for office pass
Unless we're raised above the Mass?'

'Besides, all things that are to God belong:
In seeing them as ours, you're wrong.
We hold in trust, a trust which we discharge
To benefit the Mass at large.
Language, law, and education
We extend throughout our nation,
And take the teachings of our Lord
To needy souls here and abroad.'

* * * * * * * * *

These worthy men who kneel down to receive
Now start to fade, and take their leave.
Quietly, the Man Apart his posture breaks
And Dreamscape after Dreamscape makes.
And soon in sequence there appear
Those whose accompaniment is fear,

Those Man and Nature both confound
As into dust their lives they pound.

These Dreamscapes span the centuries, and tell
How freemen into bondage fell.
Meanwhile, the Man Apart moves to assign
The blame attached to their decline.
A Reeve he summons, who relates
How Law one's civil rights instates,
But also shows what Law can mean
When Golden Ones fine-tune their scheme.

'Where on the social ladder one did stand
Was linked to tenure of one's land,
And hence the type of services one gave
Showed others how they should behave.
Thus if by chance they you should slay,
The 'Wergild' or 'Man-Price' they'd pay
Ignored by custom your renown,
And decreased as your rank went down.'

'Existing codes enjoined your kith and kin
To seek revenge through thick and thin,
And private blood-feuds generations long
Often ensued to right a wrong.
The coming of the King's own peace
Meant such vendettas had to cease:
Central controls had to ensure
No-one would dare the Law ignore.'

'And surly Churls, who formed the peasantry,
Were first by Law considered free.
We Golden Ones worked out this could be changed
If dues and taxes were arranged
To slowly sap their wherewithal
Until to villeinage they'd crawl.
Their servitude would then replace
That of the Thralls, a dying race.'

* * * * * * * * *

'Meanwhile, it was our enemies without
Who brought an English State about.
For soon came Northmen, who, by battles won,
Reduced the English Kings to one.
And once the Danelaw they'd proclaimed
Had been by Wessex Kings reclaimed,
Then future Kings could rightly say
That o'er all England they held sway.'

'But shortly, other Danes began to raid
And Ethelred them Danegeld paid;
And afterwards there came one King Canute,
Who also Norway thought to loot.
To give his Kingship more support,
Earldoms to prominence he brought,
But these the Godwin family spawned
Who showed they Law and Kingship scorned.'

'Thus Godwin, over-starred by King Canute,
Later determined to dispute
Those Norman tendencies King Edward taught
To both the English Church and Court.
So he his lawful King defied,
And rightly then to exile hied,
But soon returned with arms and fleet
And forced his King his words to eat.'

'The lingering death-throes of old Royalties
Did not destroy old loyalties,
And conjoined lands amassed by Earl and Thane
Added an even greater bane.
Scions with jealousies in-born,
Nobles too mighty to be shorn,
And ethnic Danes who loved their own
Were all to personal interests prone.'

'And English freemen found to their distress
That year by year they'd less and less.
In war they served, and paid the taxes due:
In peace they worked, war to renew.
Forays swift, famed for fires and swords,
Made Churls commend themselves to Lords,
And that long-term process started
Through which they and land were parted.'

* * * * * * * * *

SECTION 5

POSTSCRIPT: THE END OF DREAMSCAPE HISTORY

Dreamscapes and Reeve now finally retreat.
The Man Apart then takes a seat.
He's tired, but still proceeds to vent his spleen
On these sly Golden Ones I've seen.
'Surely, they had to be relieved
Of wealth and power they had received.
Their greed o'er Reason had prevailed,
And insecurity entailed.'

'They knew plutocracies create unease
In those whose liberties they seize,
And National Unity will not inspire
When living standards are thought dire.
Yet they stayed blithely unconcerned.
Their own class-consciousness they spurned,
And chose to blame domestic woes
On demonised external foes.'

'So I, Merlin, through Edward prophesied,
And signed by comet rarefied,
And then a Duke from Normandy I chose
To bring their Kingdom to a close.
Old Golden Ones he soon excised,
And feudalism he revised,

And used his Reason to create
An *Anglo-Norman Nation State.*'

Merlin began to falter as he spoke,
And vanished in a puff of smoke,
As did his scattered parchments and his cloak.
And on his going I awoke,
And instantly began to write
Our story that I've dreamed this night.
But now I see my history
May not be all it seems to be.

For memories from later years have blurred
Those that were in my genes secured:
And anachronisms, my work makes clear,
Can with false memories appear.
Thus, my wit has been deluded,
And, contrite, I have concluded
That academics may be dry
But Truth does not in Dreamscapes lie.

* * * * * * * * *